The Diverse Curriculum

The Diverse Curriculum

Bennie Kara

CORWIN
corwin.com | A Sage Company

1 Oliver's Yard
55 City Road
London EC1Y 1SP

2455 Teller Road
Thousand Oaks
California 91320
(800)233-9936

Unit No 323-333, Third Floor, F-Block
International Trade Tower
Nehru Place, New Delhi – 110 019

8 Marina View Suite 43-053
Asia Square Tower 1
Singapore 018960

Editor: Delayna Spencer
Editorial assistant: Harry Dixon
Production editor: Victoria Nicholas
Marketing manager: Dilhara Attygalle
Cover design: Wendy Scott
Typeset by: C&M Digitals (P) Ltd, Chennai, India

Library of Congress Control Number: 2024939319

British Library Cataloguing in Publication data

A catalogue record for this book is available from the British Library

ISBN 978-1-5297-7493-1
ISBN 978-1-5297-7492-4 (pbk)

This book is dedicated to all the DEI leads across the country holding difficult conversations so that the curriculum can truly allow all children to access knowledge that is truthful and nuanced.

For my girls. You are three and two right now and you have no idea what I do. But it's for you.

CONTENTS

Foreword   ix
Mary Myatt

1   The Case for Diversity in the Curriculum   1

2   Concepts in DEI Work in the Curriculum   11

3   Knowledge, Curriculum and Design   21

4   Desirable Lenses   33

5   Common Traps   43

6   Adapting the Curriculum – A School Wide Journey   55

7   Expanding the Boundaries   67

8   Parallel Stories and Paired Texts   77

9   Migrations – Linguistic, Cultural and Physical   89

10 Role Models   99

11 Countering Dominant Narratives   109

12 Case Studies Part 1 – History, Science and Maths   119

13 Case Studies Part 2 – Geography, Languages and Music   129

14 Frequently Asked Questions   137

15 Conclusion and Commitment to Action   141

Bibliography   145
Index   155

FOREWORD

Mary Myatt

Learning is never done. Learning to plan and deliver a great curriculum is also never done. I have always believed this to be the case, and even more so as a result of reading *The Diverse Curriculum*.

Bennie Kara's book is important, and it is timely: this book is important because it makes the case squarely that diversity remains a neglected strand of curriculum thinking, planning and delivery; and this book is timely, because most schools know that it is important but often aren't sure where to start or how to do it well. While there are resources available, they tend to be scattered, take time to synthesise and are often missing the rationale for this work. *The Diverse Curriculum* is the first book that brings together the arguments for a diverse curriculum and provides concrete examples to make it possible to do this well. It is a great boon to the profession.

I have been thinking about curriculum design for over 30 years and I still consider myself in the foothills of this massive and intellectually exciting domain. Reading *The Diverse Curriculum* is a reminder of how much I still need to do. I expect readers will feel the same too. This is not a blame game; we are all doing what we can, with the resources we have. However, what we don't have is an excuse not to continue learning. We are, after all, a graduate profession and we operate in the field of education, and that I argue, gives us an obligation to continue to ask questions and to develop our practice. What *The Diverse Curriculum* does is provide us with the tools to do so.

Bennie Kara presents her arguments from a position of deep experience, of teaching and leading in schools, sharing her knowledge with colleagues around the world and with authority informed by wide-ranging scholarship. She lays out the structural omissions in the National Curriculum documents which, while not ignoring the teaching about the history of the Black community, for example, nevertheless neglect to do so through any lens other than oppression. A further omission is the Matthew Arnold quote: 'The best which has been thought and said' somehow neglecting the second part of the sentence 'in the world'.

Bennie makes the case that schools can play three roles, either deliberately or inadvertently, when thinking about a diverse curriculum – they can challenge, or they can ignore, or they can perpetuate an impoverished curriculum. She observes that many schools may inadvertently fall into the 'ignore' category simply because there has not been an interrogation of how knowledge can reinforce bias.

The resulting tokenism means a diminished curriculum for all and a patronising experience for global majority pupils and anyone with one or more protected characteristic. A diminished curriculum because the long line of intellectual heritage is nowhere to be seen; a patronising experience for pupils from global majority backgrounds or with protected characteristics because their culture and identity is discussed through a single lens of Western European privilege. One way to cut through this is to consider, as Bennie argues, the diverse curriculum as a window into the rest of the world.

If, as thoughtful educators, we are intent on providing challenge to the status quo, we need the resources to help us. It could be argued that while many of us have wanted to include a wider, global lens to the content we teach, we have not done so for several reasons. For example, our own experiences of education as pupils and trainee teachers did not provide the intellectual and human landscape to widen, deepen and include other perspectives.

As Bennie says, 'We have as a profession spent less time on the knowledge, histories, art, and music of global cultures. We have done so because of our own educational experiences, of what we have been taught at university, of inheriting schemes of work, and textbooks from those who have gone before us. We are a product of our own educational experiences.'

A second reason might be that having acknowledged that there are gaps, we haven't known where to start. Now, with the publication of this remarkable book, there is no excuse.

The Diverse Curriculum sets out the scope of the work, which is substantial, but somehow Bennie makes it manageable. Through extensive examples, case studies and perspectives, this work is brought to life. For example, Christine Counsell's curriculum work for history starts with the histories of South Asian and Middle Eastern people because of their impact on the development of European cities and culture. This reverse engineering is both intellectually honest and has more resonance for all pupils, including those from a global majority heritage. Similarly, I have argued that we should go to the original sources to inform our curriculum planning and there is an excellent example of this in the Design and Technology example.

Another example, in my own work, I have often posed the question 'how many of our pupils know where zero comes from?' or 'algebra'? Because once we ask these questions, it both opens up the intellectual landscape for all pupils and honours the traditions of pupils with global majority backgrounds. I hadn't appreciated, however, the extended etymology of 'two' or of the acknowledgement of and sensitivity to gender fluidity from cultures around the world.

This cannot be left to chance. It requires intelligent leadership to provide the time, space and resources for this work. But it is so worth it, not just for our pupils but for us as professionals. When you read Bennie's account of an hour's directed time to research diversity in a current unit of work, it is stunning. I am not going to summarise here, because I don't want to give away any spoilers, you'll have to go to Chapter 6 to read it. According to Bennie, 'It was fruitful. Most of all, it was huge amounts of fun.' What could be better than that!

1

THE CASE FOR DIVERSITY IN THE CURRICULUM

In 2018, a headline caught my attention and changed the way I thought about curriculum and its role in schools. The headline stated: 'White pupils at Bath school "tied up and whipped black student for mock slave auction"' (Busby, 2018). Apart from being horrified by this act of racism, I was fascinated by the specificity of the attack. It was a racially motivated act of violence conducted by children. It was hard to comprehend how it could have happened in this day and age.

Unfortunately, some people consider racism to be a throwback to our past, as if it is not a present concern. Research by *The Guardian* in 2021 revealed that 'UK schools recorded more than 60,000 racist incidents in the past five years … as experts accused the government of failing to meet "basic safeguarding" measures by hiding the true scale of the problem' (Batty and Parveen, 2021). Racism in schools is a reality for many of our global majority children, and it cannot be ignored, especially when we consider the fact that schools are not obliged to report incidents of racist bullying. We must also consider the scale of homophobic and transphobic bullying, not just in our schools but also in our society. According to the Just Like Us independent research report 2021, LGBT+ young people are twice as likely to contemplate suicide, and Black LGBT+ young people are three times more likely (Just Like Us, 2021). Placing an intersectional lens on the figures leads to an even more alarming set of numbers. Discrimination on the basis of disability, religion and gender are still concerns in our society, and in our schools.

We do not have all the time in the world to address the social issues faced by our young people based on their identities. To create a better, fairer world, we must use the strongest, most powerful lever we have to construct a better sense of belonging for all. This is the curriculum. What we put into our curriculum is what we are saying is the most important knowledge that needs to be known to be successful in life. We say 'learn this' so that you can become a good, purposeful adult. Despite all the debate as to what a curriculum is for, many teachers would agree that it is not purely a vehicle through which young people can pass exams. It teaches us about being human, about humanity, about being humane. It teaches us about injustice and about morality. It teaches us about the past and how to be in the present and future. It is more than a set of results at the end of summative exams.

So is the curriculum fit for purpose when it comes to diversity, equity and inclusion (DEI)? Let us revisit the story I told at the start of this chapter. Four white pupils looked at their Black classmate and what did they see? They saw a person whose identity was defined by enslavement. They saw a person for whom the frame of reference for existence was defined by victimhood and oppression.

How do children develop this frame of reference? How do children acquire their understanding of the people around them? Could this incident have happened because of the way that Black history has been taught in schools?

The National Curriculum makes it clear that: 'Black history, including topics such as migration, belonging and empire, can be taught as part of the history and English curriculum in secondary schools' but 'whether pupils get to study it depends on the exam board and modules chosen by schools' (Weale et al., 2020). On the Education Hub website from our government, there is an outline of how Black history could be taught. The entire document (which is not very long) is peppered with the modal verb 'could'.

> At Key Stage 1 the curriculum requires key historical events within or beyond living memory to be taught. This could include teaching about the lives of key Black and minority ethnic historical figures such as Mary Seacole and Rosa Parks, both of whom are used as examples in the programmes of study.

> Teachers could, for example, look at Britain's transatlantic slave trade – its effects and its eventual abolition – including the successful slave-led rebellions, such as the Haitian Revolution, that eventually led to the abolition of slavery. In the UK, this could include the role played by slaves and former slaves such as Olaudah Equiano as well as the Somerset Ruling. (educationhub.blog.gov.uk, 2021)

It goes on to suggest that schools study the British role in slavery, and that they examine the lives of particular enslaved people such as Olaudah Equiano. It is not a detailed document of suggestions, but there is certainly no sense of encouragement to learn about the history of the Black community through any lens than oppression. The word 'could' creates possibility, suggests permission, allows scope. Most of us would see this as a positive, but within the scope of 'could' is also 'do not have to'. If you are not well versed in Black history, or if indeed, you do not believe that it should be taught, alongside other diverse content, then 'could' is a get-out.

So, when I consider the headline I started with above, I am not surprised that non-Black children's view of being Black is limited. There is limited scope for it in the curriculum, at least officially speaking. It often comes down to knowledgeable and interested parties to do the legwork to create a diverse and decolonised curriculum – which is not then sustained or embedded.

I do not do this work just because of that headline. I am often asked whether I do this work on curriculum leadership because of international events such as George Floyd's murder, or because of the Black Lives Matter movement. The answer is partly. I am exhausted by the racism, homophobia, misogyny and ableism I hear about, locally, nationally and globally. But there is more.

My ongoing work on diversifying and decolonising the curriculum also stems from my absolute belief that the curriculum is a window into the world. That window should be a way for our students to see the joy, the invention, the knowledge, the tragedy, the oppression, the victories, the ideas and creations of people of all backgrounds and identities. That window should also be a mirror. Let me explain the metaphor.

Professor Rudine Sims Bishop talks beautifully about books being windows, mirrors and sliding glass doors:

> Books are sometimes **windows**, offering views of worlds that may be real or imagined, familiar or strange. These windows are also **sliding glass doors**, and readers have only to walk through in imagination to become part of whatever world has been created or recreated by the author. When lighting conditions are just right, however, a window can also be a **mirror**. (Bishop, 1990: ix–xi)

She is writing about the impact of books on a child's life and sense of self. Her words can also be applied to the curriculum. The curriculum can be a window into worlds unseen, it is about seeing outside of oneself and one's immediate surroundings; the sliding door of the curriculum is the opportunities knowledge creates to be something greater, to achieve, to walk in new circles. The mirror is the way in which we make sense of knowledge – how it applies to us, how it tells our story – thereby helping us fit into the global narrative. The curriculum that is a mirror helps us find our worth.

It is not often that I turn to Michael Gove for anything, let alone as a rationale for a book about diversity in the curriculum. Yet, here I am, quoting the former Secretary of State for Education and one usually known for narrowing the scope of content in the English curriculum. He is an unlikely ally in this quest to create a truly diverse curriculum. In 2009, in a new oft-cited speech to the RSA (Royal Society for the Arts), Gove outlined his vision for education. In it, he cited Michael Oakeshott in affirming that every human being is born heir to 'an inheritance of human achievements; an inheritance of thoughts, beliefs, ideas, understandings, intellectual and practical enterprises, languages, canons, works of art, books, musical compositions and so on'. Gove (2009) went on to argue that 'Education should be a process of granting every individual their rights to that inheritance.'

I couldn't agree more. Gove's use of Oakeshott's ideas, laid out in *The Voice of Liberal Learning* were never meant to be interpreted as a clarion call for diversity in the curriculum (Oakeshott, 1989). I am more than happy, believe me, to take Gove at his word.

Milem et al. (2005) cite Bickel (1998) in which he 'argues that the belief that exposing students to a wider range of opinions improves the quality of those students' intellectual advancement can be traced back to John Stuart Mill's famous 1859 essay,

"On Liberty." In that essay, Mill argues that popular opinions must be submitted to the "marketplace of ideas" and suggests that when perceptions are narrowed by the limits or biases of experience, geography, education, or class, they become the basis of judgment and social policy, and true social advancement is ostensibly compromised.'

In short, we need to broaden perspectives in order for social change to occur.

Do I believe that the racist bullies of the headline I started with would have behaved any differently if they had access to a better curriculum? I cannot be certain. Do I want to believe that they may have thought twice about it had they understood that their Black peer was their equal in worth, if their understanding of him and his history was more rounded? I want to believe that. I want to believe that our education system can do better to show not just the presence of diverse identities, but also the weight of worth of those identities in our societies, past, present and future.

Why are We Here?

The fact that you are reading this book suggests to me one of two things: either you are absolutely on board with the idea that the curriculum as it stands needs greater diversity, or perhaps you need convincing. In either case, to reinforce your enthusiasm, or to provide you with a rationale, perhaps it is important, then, to question why this book needs to exist at all.

We must first turn our attention to the ways in which social forces, international news, domestic politics and the growing impact of a global pandemic have impacted upon our perceptions, and the perceptions of young people, of the world we live in.

Here comes the neuroscience.

The Role of Bias in Society

We are designed to survive, as a species. Our biological and neurological evolution is predicated on making sure we are not in danger. Dr Pragya Agarwal, behavioural scientist and author of *Sway: Unravelling Unconscious Bias* outlines the need for humans to create 'in-groups' and 'out-groups' (Agarwal, 2020). We have a heightened awareness of these 'out-groups' because they might pose danger. How do we decide on these 'out-groups'? Historically, we would have used our ancient human tribal instincts. Our brains have kept these instincts: we absorb information about people, situations, events and feelings and we accumulate a view. Agarwal cites three theories of what our brains do with that information. For brevity, I shall examine just one.

In 1979, Daniel Kahneman and Amos Tversky examined the brain's processes in making judgements, considering probability and the way that we store and use information. Their findings, called *representative heuristics*, suggested that our brains take in information at such a rate that it is necessary for us to create shortcuts in order to make sense of and use the information. In this circumstance, speed is much more important than accuracy. We develop cognitive errors and biases this way. We create stereotypes (Agarwal, 2020).

How is this relevant to prejudice? Ever heard the phrase rubbish in, rubbish out? This concept applies to the kind of information we get about people – how our representative heuristics are formed. In our earlier stages of development, we are primed to believe certain things about certain groups of people. This is a natural consequence of soaking up information from outside of ourselves, you cannot stop it happening, you cannot adjust in the moment if you are very young and so some ideas become entrenched, repeated and therefore part of our social consciousness. Inaccurate assumptions can be benign, however they can lead to the formation of harmful stereotypes. It might be the case that inaccurate information leads to the belief that certain groups are more responsible for crime in our society or that certain religions are somehow harmful and at odds with British culture. It might be the case that inaccurate information leads to gender stereotypes that persist into adulthood.

Where and how do young people form their opinions of the world around them and of groups of people? If young people are truly sponges – and the research would suggest that they are – of course, they will start forming inaccurate assumptions about identity, race, gender, sexuality, early on in their lives.

Children take information from a range of sources, often unquestioning, because of course they trust the adults in their lives to tell them the truth. But when that truth is influenced by inaccurate assumptions and inaccurate information that is believed unquestioningly, children are of course susceptible to developing a worldview that is limited in scope, that is difficult to unpick and in some cases may lead to damaging experiences if those worldviews are repeated. So in many ways, work on diversifying and colonising the curriculum is an act of compassion and an exercise in developing critical thinking. Put simply, we must ensure students have the widest access to the widest range of information about people, places, cultures and histories, so that they may make decisions with as three-dimensional a worldview as possible.

Inaccurate assumptions can appear in a variety of forms. One of these is called the Halo Effect. Edward Thorndike coined this term to describe how we make assumptions about people based on one characteristic, or experience (Thorndike, 1920). He outlined how, for example, a person's perceived attractiveness might lead one to assume that their whole personality is good. One trait equals the whole of our perception. Equally, the opposite might be true. If we perceive one negative trait about someone, then we assume that all their traits are negative.[1]

School staff may find themselves falling prey to the halo effect. If they believe a child is well-behaved, staff might also assume that the same child is bright and capable of high outcomes. Children can also make assumptions based on outward appearances. If

---

[1] It must be noted however that Thorndike is a problematic figure in the world of education. He believed in eugenics and was noted for his racist and sexist views. Some institutions have removed their connection with him. The halo effect idea is not related to his racist and sexist views.

a child perceives a physical disability to be unattractive, they may go on to assume that that person with a disability has other negative traits.

In fact, perceived level of attractiveness is often a marker of how we determine someone's likeability and, according to research, attractiveness and persuasion are linked (Gordon et al., 2013). This has implications on all sorts of levels: your ability to persuade someone that you will be a good candidate for a job; your ability to advocate for yourself and your family; your ability to be 'believed' on a stage or elsewhere. The danger here lies in our society's perceptions of what attractive is. We are conditioned to believe that lighter complexions, finer features, physical fitness, able bodies and silken hair are the pinnacle of beauty standards (Bagalini, 2020). Therefore, if we are conditioned to believe that anyone who does not look like this is unattractive, we may also then believe other negative things about them: their abilities, their values, their behaviours, their morals, their actions.

Growing up - Inaccurate Assumptions into Concrete Beliefs

To compound early assumptions, young people also soak up their family and community views about marginalised groups (even if they come from marginalised groups themselves). In one of the schools I worked in, I was faced with a child who was using extremely negative language about Muslim women. When I asked him if he understood the terms he was using were unacceptable, he replied: 'That's what my mum calls them.'

Examining the potential correlation between parental prejudice and children's development of prejudice, Sabine Pirchio and colleagues (2018) found that 'children's prejudice may be rooted in the automatic behavior and implicit social influence processes enacted by their significant adults, more than in what parents explicitly think (and likely say) about ethnically different people to their children'.

Of course, there is a strong possibility that children are going to repeat what is said in the home, sometimes without thought. But as those children grow up, and they are faced with a tide of information about particular groups of people in society, that information will only serve to reinforce problematic ideas that have taken root in the home. While the internet is a wonderful thing, we must examine the impact it has on how children experience the world around them.

Technological Shifts and Knowledge

Hope Not Hate, a charitable trust that researches hatred and racism in society, published 'Young People in the Time of Covid-19: A Fear and Hope Study of 16-24 Year Olds' in 2020. In it, the researcher Rosie Carter outlines the prevalence of conspiracy theory belief amongst young people, as facilitated by social media. She states: 'While just 29%

of 16–24 year olds say that they watch the news daily, large numbers of young people, especially young men, are consuming alternative media sources online, with some accessing extreme, conspiratorial or misogynistic content online.' She goes on to outline how: 'Worryingly, 14% of young people, and 19% of young men, think it is true that Jewish people have an unhealthy control over the world's banking system. Moreover, 15% of young people, and 20% of young men, say that is true that the official account of the Nazi Holocaust is a lie and the number of Jews killed by the Nazis during World War II has been exaggerated on purpose' (Carter, 2019: 9). Of course, we can see that statistics show that these kind of beliefs are in the minority; however, we can also see that even these figures are a concern – especially if they go unchallenged in schools.

Our students live in a society that has undergone a distinct transition. It could be argued that our students are exposed to the world in a way that I certainly was not as a child. To form my views, I listened to my parents, spoke with my friends, watched the television. To a certain extent, that stream of information was fairly limited. With the advent of the internet and instant access to video streaming, children have at their fingertips a world of information – all at once wonderful and terrifying in its unfiltered form. It could be argued that we, as teachers, as parents, lack the mechanisms to truly help our students understand this world and process society in a useful and supportive way.

Consider the impact of algorithms on a child's absorption of information. They might start by searching for information on the Holocaust. How many clicks away from anti-Semitic material are they? In 2021, Hope Not Hate reiterated that platforms such as TikTok and Instagram can be used as gateways to anti-Semitic material (Sky News, n.d.). Alongside this, research on convictions for radicalisation revealed that online radicalisation of young people was on the rise (Kenyon et al., 2021). Our young people are far more subject to the dangers of social media than we are as adults; if we do not in the first instance challenge the content they may have accessed and then provide counter-information, then perhaps we are guilty of putting our heads in the proverbial sand.

As teachers, we know how important it is for young people to feel like they belong in social circles with their peers. Comfort, feeling like you fit in, feeling that you have things in common with peers – all are part of growing up. It makes sense then that agreement on ideas about race, gender, sexuality and so on might be replicated and propagated in the social groups of the children in our schools. This is not to say that children will be in blind agreement with all views, but there is a risk of replication of negative ideas within friendship groups. After all, it takes a lot of strength and confidence to disagree with friends at that age, especially if you want to fit in, feel accepted and have a semblance of popularity.

The Role of Schools

That leaves school as the final source of information from which students can form their viewpoints, or indeed, have their deep-rooted views challenged. It is inevitable that we stand as a barrier against racist, sexist, homophobic and ableist ideas – because we are responsible not just for introducing knowledge, but also shaping the ability of students to be critical about the knowledge they gain.

Schools can play three roles, either deliberately or inadvertently, when thinking about a diverse curriculum. What do they look like? Table 1.1 gives an overview.

Table 1.1 The role of schools in diversifying the curriculum

Challenge	Actively seek to counter dominant narratives about people, places and ideas	Highlighting examples of indigenous knowledge in the curriculum and advocating for change
Ignore	Deny there is any need for change, preserve the status quo	Continuing to teach a Eurocentric curriculum that is male dominated
Perpetuate	Actively seek to reinforce prejudice through the curriculum	Teaching that LGBT+ people are unacceptable

Fortunately, it is rare to see a school institution actively reinforcing prejudice thanks to the Equality Act and the Public Sector Equality Duty. But many schools may inadvertently fall into the 'ignore' category simply because there has not been an interrogation of how knowledge can reinforce bias.

Is it important to do this work in all schools? Even when the majority of the students are white? Arguably, it's even more important. It is then incumbent upon us to start the process of 'demystifying the Other'. This is particularly important when the school environment is monocultural. Milem et al., drawing on the work of Kanter (1977), reveal that where there is a majority white population in an education setting, there is a greater chance of tokenism. While Milem at al. are writing and researching from a US context, there is clearly a lesson to be learned about how difference is delineated in majority white settings, where they cite Hurtado et al., (1994): 'campuses with high proportions of white students provide limited opportunities for cross-racial interaction and restrict student learning experiences across social and cultural lines' (Hurtado et al., 1994, cited in Milem et al., 2005).

A diverse curriculum provides here a window into the rest of the world.

A Note on Neutrality

As teachers, we often find ourselves wanting to follow rules. We are very good at colouring within the lines. Staying politically impartial is a concern that many teachers raise with me whenever I deliver training on diversifying the curriculum. It is not hard to see how these fears are stoked. When delivering a speech to the Heritage Foundation in the US, Oliver Dowden, a British MP, denounced what he deemed to be 'painful woke psychodrama' and declared that it has been made clear 'that it is illegal [it isn't actually] to teach the concept of "white privilege" as though it were undisputed fact' (Dowden, 2022).

So what does it mean to be politically impartial? Guidance from the Department for Education in the United Kingdom seems to cover a lot of ground and simultaneously manages to be unspecific in most areas. The key information is as follows:

- The guidance is not legally binding in introducing new duties, but exists to reinforce existing laws about not 'promoting politically partisan views'.
- Schools have a responsibility to ensure that they are not inviting groups with extremist views to talk to their students. This means that groups have to be vetted so that there is no encouragement to overthrow democratic processes.
- While some historical events do not need to be considered in light of political impartiality, the teaching of empire does because it has been seen as controversial more recently. Empire needs to be taught in a balanced manner.
- Partisan political views on Israel and Palestine need to be given context and handled sensitively. It is argued in the guidelines that some views may be contested.
- Significant figures can be presented factually, and in light of what they are most known for.
- Homophobia can be challenged.
- When engaging in debate about recent events involving Black Lives Matter, it is important not to engage in arguments about defunding the police.

So does this mean that we cannot diversify the curriculum? Not at all. It means that we have to do what we have always done as teachers: research our subjects, consider the intention and balance of our teaching, check in with the guidelines, check in with our leadership teams and take Nadhim Zawahi's words into consideration:

> I don't want there to be any barriers – real or perceived – to teachers' vital work in this space, which is why I am reinforcing that no subject is off-limits in the classroom, as long as it is treated in an age-appropriate way, with sensitivity and respect, and without promoting contested theories as fact. (Adams, 2022)

There are aspects of the diverse curriculum that you may need to consider carefully when deciding what to teach and how. If in doubt, seek advice first.

Ultimately, we have to remember that building a curriculum that embraces, celebrates, highlights and foregrounds diversity is an act of equity and allyship. It is something we can all do, daily.

.... **REFLECTION QUESTIONS**

- What role does the curriculum play in creating a child's worldview?
- How does it shape understanding of identity, historically and in the present?
- How has the National Curriculum created space for the study of global majority culture and varying identities?
- How do we combat the way in which biases are formed using the curriculum?

....

2

CONCEPTS IN DEI WORK IN THE CURRICULUM

If you are reading this and you are suddenly struck by the moral imperative and social imperative to create a diverse curriculum, you may also be struck with the acute understanding that you are time limited and that you do not have infinite resources.

So how do we go about ensuring that this work happens and that we are not burned out by our quest to fix all of society's ills? Fortunately we have at our disposal the ultimate tool through which we can make huge differences to our children's understanding of the world they live in. The curriculum, in all of its sprawling glory, is our pathway to a better understanding of difference, of identity, and of the histories and cultures who have traditionally been missed out of the story over the centuries. It is the curriculum that is our act of allyship and equity. It is the most powerful tool to demonstrate how knowledge in all its forms is important. What we choose to put in front of children is deemed the most important knowledge of our existence; so of course when we choose wisely and equitably the content, the stories, the histories, the music and the culture we foreground, we are explaining to children how to be human in our society.

In order to create a diverse curriculum, educators need to work on the literacy of diversity. The more we know, the more we are aware of how to reshape the curriculum to be diverse and inclusive.

If you are looking at concepts on DEI, you might want to peruse the following books, as well as those cited in the chapter:

- *Why Are All the Black Kids Sitting Together in the Cafeteria?* – Beverley Daniel Tatum
- *How to be an Anti-Racist* – Ibram X Kendi
- *Outrageous! The Story of Section 28 and Britain's Battle for LGBT Education* – Paul Baker
- *Brit(ish): Ideas about Race, Identity and Belonging* – Afua Hirsch
- *The Wretched of the Earth* – Franz Fanon

- *Trans Historical: Gender Plurality before the Modern* – Eds. Greta LaFleur, Masha Rasolnikov and Anna Klosowka
- *Demystifying Disability* – Emily Ladau

Allyship

Allyship is an active process in which one advocates for someone outside of their own identity. The emphasis is firmly on the word 'active'. Poornima Luthra, in the *Harvard Business Review*, outlines four aspects of allyship that are vital in ensuring that allyship is not just performative.

- Deep curiosity in which we must interrogate our own and others' intersectional identities, where reflection on difference is focused not just in the now, but in historical context too.
- Honest introspection about the ways in which our brains construct bias and how we act upon this information daily.
- Humble acknowledgement of how much privilege plays a part in our existence, with a view to using that privilege to support others.
- Empathetic engagement through which we can ask questions, listen to lived experience and challenge – what Luthra terms 'termite biases' or microaggressions. (Luthra, 2022)

Anti-Racism

Anti-racism is a key concept in DEI work. It is important to define what it is and what it is not, as a concept and as an action, and in relation to education and the curriculum. For this, I turn to Ibram X Kendi (2019: 17), who tells us: 'To be an antiracist is to set lucid definitions of racism/antiracism, racist/antiracist policies, racist/anti-racist ideas, racist/antiracist people.' The lucid defining needs to start with what our understanding of racism is. The United Nations definition provides a starting point in its Declaration on Race and Racial Prejudice:

> Racism includes racist ideologies, prejudiced attitudes, discriminatory behaviour, structural arrangements and institutionalized practices resulting in racial inequality as well as the fallacious notion that discriminatory relations between groups are morally and scientifically justifiable; it is reflected in discriminatory provisions in legislation or regulations and discriminatory practices as well as in anti-social beliefs and acts; it hinders the development of its victims, perverts those who practise it, divides nations internally, impedes international co-operation and gives rise to political tensions between peoples; it is contrary to the fundamental principles of international law and, consequently, seriously disturbs international peace and security. (United Nations, 1978)

This definition does not encompass the sociological explorations of race as construct, race as a marker of hierarchy (what Boaventura de Sousa Santos calls the 'abyssal line'), or indeed how race, race science and colonialism are intrinsically linked. There is also a need to explore how racism exists on a variety of levels (Figure 2.1).

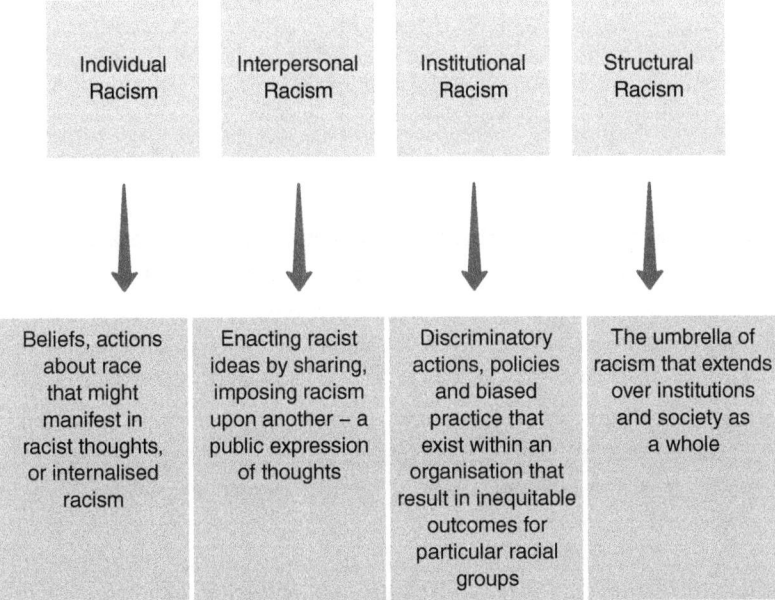

Figure 2.1   Scales of racism

Adapted from Smithsonian (2019)

To be able to explore racism thoroughly, I have included key texts at the end of this chapter that allow you to delve deeper into ideas connected with racism itself.

Kendi points out that anti-racism is not the same as being 'not-racist'. The opposite of racist is anti-racist. The Welsh government have recently made a commitment to anti-racism and define action as such:

- Working towards breaking down systems of racial oppression and discrimination (recognising them in the curriculum and considering the countering actions)
- Involving more than just holding non-prejudiced views or avoiding acts of racism (challenging racist ideas in the curriculum openly with a view to the historical record and roots of thinking)
- Challenging and confronting racist beliefs, behaviours and institutional structures (seeking to situate an anti-racist curriculum as part of the culture of your school)
- Recognising your own privilege and understanding how it contributes to systemic racism (decentring yourself in the creation of the anti-racist curriculum) (www. gov.wales, 2024).

The words in parentheses are mine, not the Welsh government's. It is important to frame concept against curriculum design and ensure there is a way to move forward practically.

Equality vs Equity

Howard Schultz, the former CEO of Starbucks, said at a town-hall event on Tuesday night that he doesn't see colour when it comes to race. Schultz indicated that 'as somebody who grew up in a very diverse background as a young boy in the projects, I didn't see color as a young boy and I honestly don't see color now'. (Asare, n.d.)

When I was a teenager, I had a sticker on my bedside table in stark black and white, with the words 'All Different, All Equal' in large bold letters. At the time, my precocious 15-year-old self had no real understanding of the terminology of social justice. If only someone had come along early in my development as a human being on this earth and explained to me why 'All Different, All Equal' was a glib and unhelpful slogan.

Equality, in the 1990s, when I was in my formative years, was exemplified by statements like these. After all, who can forget being told by Michael Jackson in 1991, 'it doesn't matter if you're black or white'? The line seemed so positive, so simple and pertinent. We were learning that people had equal status. But of course the line – and our society then – both suffered from a common misconception that possibly led to an entire generation of people declaring that they 'don't see colour'.

Not seeing colour, and the implications for a person of colour in our society, is a failing that leads to generalisations, misunderstanding of privilege and microaggression. When someone says to me 'I don't see you as an Asian person, you're just like everyone else' (or some variation of this), I hear the rejection of my identity, a lack of acknowledgement of how my identity has shaped my world and a lack of understanding of the joys and delights of my culture, and the hurdles and barriers I have faced.

Because of course it does matter if you are black or white. Or East Asian, or like me, East African Asian. It matters in the way you are treated, the amount of money you make, the opportunities you have access to, the way in which you are perceived by others, the way institutions see you, the way your body is treated, and in the ways in which you are valued by others.

Knowing the difference between equality and equity is vital in understanding how to create a diverse curriculum (Table 2.1). Fundamentally, equality is an end point; equity should be seen as the process by which we reach equality. Equality assumes we are all the same, that we all have the same starting points, whereas equity recognises that we are different, that we are born into societies with advantage and disadvantage, that we need mitigating factors to allow our individual identities to flourish in society.

Table 2.1 Equality vs equity

Equality	Equity
Assumes everyone is the same and should be treated as such	Understands that people are not the same and have individual needs
Ignores the impact of privilege and disadvantage on life experiences	Recognises the impact of disadvantage
Exists as a byproduct of a just society	Seeks to address injustice
Exacerbates existing disadvantage by ignoring individual needs	Levels the playing field
Disregards historical marginalisation	Mitigates historical marginalisation

When people question why there is a lack of an International Men's Day, they are demonstrating that they do not understand what equity means. Men have been afforded rights and protections above those of women, historically and in the present day. So why would they need to have a day in which their rights and their safety and their promotion is placed front and centre in people's minds? They have a different starting point; one that means they have advantages that women have not had. If we take an equitable approach, we are saying that women need something that men do not – they need a day in which we highlight and promote the rights of women in order for men and women to become more equal in our society. The complaint – why do I not have the same thing as you? – is akin to an able-bodied person campaigning for a ramp because a person in a wheelchair has one.

As teachers, we are more adept at thinking equitably than most. Our job requires us to recognise the different starting points of children in the classroom – some have special education needs and disabilities (SEND) and require more scaffolding of the work in order for them to achieve the same goals as students without additional needs. Some students have physical disabilities that mean they need to sit in particular places in the classroom in order to access work better. This is thinking equitably – thinking about how we mitigate disadvantage into creating a fairer space. It is not difficult then to understand that society works in exactly the same way. We are to understand that nationally and internationally, there are people with disadvantage who need more support, more money, more intervention, more physical protections than those who are advantaged.

If we consider how this works in the curriculum, we are compelled at this point then to spend more time thinking about content that represents the diverse population than we do about more traditional, white Western European content than we have previously. We have as a profession spent less time on the knowledge, histories, art, and music of global cultures. We have done so because of our own educational experiences, of what we have been taught at university, of inheriting schemes of work and textbooks from those who have gone before us. We are a product of our own educational experiences.

We know how to teach Dickens, but now we need to spend a bit more time thinking about how to incorporate and teach texts by writers of colour, as relevant to the curriculum sequence we are creating. The mitigation here is our time and effort – our thought processes focused on content that enriches children's understanding of the nation's cultural history.

When we make a conscious effort to consider a diverse curriculum, we are acknowledging there is a gap in the current one, that the story is not complete and hasn't been complete for centuries.

Decolonisation vs Diversity

The difference between diversity and decolonisation needs to be explored. Sometimes the two words are used interchangeably and fundamentally this is a misunderstanding of their very individual purposes in DEI work.

Decolonisation as a concept is highly academic and centres around the dismantling of structures and systems associated with colonisation. It challenges the imbalance of power created by colonisation and seeks to imagine a world in which those structures and systems do not exist. It is very much centred on race and culture and the impact of empire and its capitalist mechanisms. According to Krauss (2018), it involves 'questioning and unpacking how colonial and hegemonic structures of power continue to produce contemporary inequalities, and reflecting on how these highly unequal structures can be addressed'.

In the curriculum, this means holding an awareness of how colonialism has impacted on the knowledge we choose as valuable and to actively redress the balance of where knowledge comes from and who has originated it, as far as it is possible to know this. It means actively making different choices about what we choose to teach, and indeed, how we choose to teach. In her practice in Canada, Eugenia Zurosky, Associate Professor of English and Cultural Studies at McMaster University, asks her students: 'where do you know from?' as a method of establishing a decolonised classroom by including the perspectives of the students in the room (MAI, 2020).

Diversity is often seen as less impactful than decolonisation work. While it may not challenge colonial thinking directly, we do need to consider the ways in which diversity can be addressed using a decolonial lens. Diversity is often intersectional, encompasses aspects of decolonisation whilst acknowledging the needs and challenges faced by other protected characteristics. This doesn't mean that diversity work is somehow glossing over the challenges faced by those who are experiencing racism, or those who feel that colonial structures still exist and serve to prevent power from being redistributed. Diversity work can be engaged with how power represses those with protected characteristics and to imagine the world in which our individual identities are catered for, and in which we meet people where they are, in order to treat them equitably.

Diversity is no less important than decolonisation. Diversity is different in that it encompasses the recognition, acceptance and celebration of differences among individuals or groups, including differences in race, ethnicity, gender, sexuality, religion and ability, as well as in other protected characteristics. It seeks to emphasise the existence and value of varied perspectives, identities and experiences within a society or community. It can be argued that the goal of diversity initiatives is to create inclusive environments that respect and value these differences. It involves promoting representation, equality and opportunities for marginalised or underrepresented groups.

In the curriculum, this means exploring the ways in which we make space for people and ideas from different social backgrounds and identities. On the very surface, we are compelled to consider who is made voiceless and erased by the current curriculum and to redress that balance. In doing so, we can move from a curriculum that is centred on, and seems to value only, the white, Eurocentric concept of knowledge through to better representation and a fairer distribution of power.

The terms can be seen as interconnected in many ways. Decolonising the curriculum often intersects with diversifying the curriculum, as decolonisation can involve recognising and embracing diverse cultural perspectives. In the end, both a decolonised and diverse curriculum aims to create more equitable and inclusive societies.

Intersectionality

Intersectionality is a concept first articulated by Kimberlé Crenshaw in the late 1980s, referring to the interconnected nature of social categorisations such as race, class, gender, sexuality, ability and other forms of identity. Crenshaw suggested that these identities do not exist separately from each other but rather intersect or overlap, creating unique experiences of discrimination and privilege for individuals who hold multiple marginalised identities. Crenshaw went on to write about the concept of intersectionality in detail in 'Mapping the Margins: Intersectionality, Identity Politics, and Violence against Women of Color' (Crenshaw, 2020).

Crenshaw initially introduced this concept concerning the legal system's failure to address the unique experiences of Black women facing both racial and gender discrimination. The idea has since expanded to recognise that individuals' experiences cannot be understood solely through the lens of a single identity, emphasising the need to consider the multiple overlaps of identity when analysing social issues.

Intersectionality is crucial because it highlights the complexity of social structures and power dynamics. It acknowledges that individuals experience different forms of oppression or privilege based on the combination of their identities, which can significantly impact their access to opportunities, resources and societal treatment. In *Intersectionality as Critical Social Theory* (2019), Patricia Hill Collins expands on the concept of intersectionality as a critical tool for understanding power dynamics and social inequalities. It is explored too by Audre Lorde in *Sister Outsider* (1984), her collection of essays examining the intersections of race, gender and sexuality, and serves to highlight the complexities and interconnections among various forms of oppression (Lorde, 1984). We see this deftly explored in bell hooks' *Ain't I a Woman? Black Women and*

Feminism (1981), where hooks explores the intersection of race, gender and class and their impacts on Black women's experiences within feminist movements.

For our practice, this means recognising the ways in which marginalised identities show up in the curriculum. Is it easy to apply broad brush strokes to identities in statements such as 'Black history is a part of our curriculum', or that 'women are well represented in our curriculum', when the reality is that both identity descriptors in those statements do not allow for nuance, or overlap. For there to be a truly intersectional approach, we must seek to break those statements down further by asking:

- How can we include the voices, histories, art, culture and experiences of more specific groups of people from different backgrounds?
- How can we ensure that the presence of women in the curriculum is not limited to white women, but women from the global majority?
- Where is it possible to highlight the achievements of global majority people with disabilities?
- How can we ensure that the discussion of LGBTQ+ people includes people from different religions or nationalities?

Demystification of the 'Other'

Students with different identities will be placed next to each other in our classrooms and go on to encounter these differences later in life. It is essential that they learn through the curriculum that 'Othering' is problematic. In the wake of 9/11 and the subsequent wave of Islamophobia that followed, analyses of language used about Muslims showed that an 'us-vs-them' mentality was a reality. Said, in *The Colonial Present: Afghanistan, Palestine and Iraq* (2004: 24), stated:

> To build a conceptual framework around a notion of Us-versus-Them is, in effect, to pretend that the principal consideration is epistemological and natural – our civilization is known and accepted, theirs is different and strange – whereas, in fact, the framework separating us from them is belligerent, constructed, and situational.

This 'tribalism' (a term that is still used in the context of Said's work) is an interesting lens through which we can examine the curriculum. How far does the curriculum in its current form encourage the following?

- An us-vs-them mentality: where we have diversity in silo-form in the curriculum, we can inadvertently exacerbate existing divisions in society. Encounters with identities that are put on a metaphorical plinth may serve only to highlight 'different', as opposed to 'usual'.

- In-group favouritism: a curriculum that only belongs to one group of people may highlight division and lead to social silos, because young people may grow up to believe that 'their people' are the only ones worth valuing.
- Social division and conflict: a curriculum that is monocultural, heteronormative and ableist creates hierarchies of importance and value that may in turn lead to increased division.
- Prejudice and discrimination: a curriculum that erases the voices of the marginalised may result in a cycle of misinformation and prejudice remaining unbroken.
- Resistance to change: a curriculum that only values the status quo may result in young people never gaining an imperative for change, thereby perpetuating existing injustices.

We can see examples of this kind of social division and the us-vs-them mentality in our schools, simply by observing how our young people interact. Beverley Daniel Tatum talks extensively about the phenomenon in *Why Are All the Black Kids Sitting Together in the Cafeteria?* (1997). She explores the notion of group identity and stereotype threat. The concept, as outlined by Claude Steele, suggests that group identity and stereotype threat are very much a risk factor for underperformance of marginalised groups that are undervalued and underrepresented in schools. In essence, once we have group identities that are associated with negative stereotypes, those young people will be more anxious about how they behave, how they work and how they present in a school setting because they do not want to be the stereotype that is laid out for them as an identity marker.

Tatum explores the idea that social messages (and if we extrapolate, curricular messages) define how young people see themselves. She explains that prejudice, misinformation and erasure impact on how young people interact with each other. It is a stark reminder that we have a responsibility to counter the us-vs-them mentality and to provide more nuanced and more positive examples of how diversity benefits our society, and how we can learn to interact better in the future.

Emotional Tax

What happens if you are constantly on guard against bias? If the curriculum never seeks to redress the inequities in our society, there is a heavy price to pay for being seen as different-negative. The term 'emotional tax' may have been coined in 2018 by the global non-profit organisation Catalyst, in which they defined the psychological burden of difference that is not valued in the workplace (Travis and Thorpe-Moscon, 2018). They drew on the work of Himmelstein et al. (2014), where the authors examined hypervigilance in marginalised Black groups in the US.

What is this emotional tax and how does it manifest in schools? It relates to the burden or cost that young people might face when recognising that they need to be on guard, or vigilant against prejudice. There are many ways in which this emotional tax might appear:

1 Identity-based stress – relates to marginalised identities who are navigating bias, stereotypes, microaggressions and discriminatory behaviours.
2 Code-switching and managing reactions – relates to the fear of not fitting in or having to curb emotions for fear of being seen as a stereotype.
3 Emotional drain – leads to increased stress, anxiety and exhaustion that impacts on wellbeing, which may lead to decreased engagement in school life and work.

How does a curriculum that is diverse in nature alleviate this emotional tax? Firstly, it teaches that people of varying identities are valued as integral members of our society. It reinforces the idea that difference is 'usual' and allows for that elusive demystification of those who have been traditionally Othered. There is also the possibility that a diverse curriculum might seek to highlight racism, homophobia, Islamophobia and so on, and thus build awareness of how we as individuals can serve our diverse communities better.

REFLECTION QUESTIONS

- Could I explain the concepts in this chapter to someone with no knowledge of them?
- How can I link DEI concepts with the imperative to act on diversifying the curriculum?
- What 'diversity literacy' gaps exist in my organisation?
- How can an organisation encourage staff to develop their diversity literacy?

3
KNOWLEDGE, CURRICULUM AND DESIGN

To create a curriculum that is truly diverse and avoids tokenism is a challenge for any teacher. When considering how best to create that curriculum, it helps to have in mind some underlying principles that guide us through the misconceptions and errors that can take place.

Firstly, we must take into account the tokenistic nature of previous efforts to diversify the curriculum. This is by no means anyone's fault; the curriculum has always been a mechanism in which content has been influenced by personal preferences, prior knowledge and comfort zones. The resulting journey has been littered with good intentions, with diverse content smattered randomly throughout units of work and long-term plans.

It is critical that we as teachers have a detailed understanding of both curriculum design and diverse subject matter. Consider this: when introducing a new unit of work, or adjusting lesson sequences, what process do you go through in deciding where it goes and what goes in it? Is the process driven by an individual's choice or is there a meaningful discussion of how that content fits into the sequence of learning? Why do we choose what we choose? In some cases it may be true that the content you choose is driven by the National Curriculum, which of course is hugely important. But the nuances of lesson-by-lesson design are far more reflective of our individual preferences. We might also consider what order the content goes in, and the rationale behind what is where in the long-term sequence of learning.

In short, we need to consider 'how' learning happens, 'what' is being taught and 'how' to design a curriculum when it comes to diverse narratives.

What is Schema and How is it Formed?

The term 'schema' is said to have first been used by Frederick Bartlett, drawing on his interpretations of Henry Head's work on body schema. It took on life as a concept in Piagetian education theory.

To explain how schemas work, Piaget (1976) outlined the following:

- We develop our knowledge and understanding when new information is added or assimilated into current, existing schemas.
- When we cannot easily integrate new information, it creates cognitive dissonance.
- Schemas are forced to change/accommodate this new information.

It is often used to describe how the brain accumulates knowledge, from baseline, simple concepts to complex understanding of a topic. For example, we may understand that cats are animals at the most basic level, but as we continue the process of acquiring new knowledge, we 'attach' additional ideas like cats are mammals and cats are sacred and symbolic in Egyptian culture. We are building the complex web of information, our brains tying the new to the old, adjusting position, importance, relevance as we go.

We form schema about the society we live in too. The concept of society and the people in it grows as we move from childhood into adulthood. This 'social' or 'cultural' schema is far more vulnerable to inaccuracy and misinformation than our schema about cats, because our view of society is subject to others' opinions, a multitude of explanations, a more theoretical basis than the facts about cats. So this social schema, the knowledge acquired and organised by our brains, may need to be unpicked as well as developed.

Consider how a very young child develops schema about disability. Some of pre-school children's earliest encounters with disability come in the form of disfigurement and limb difference in Disney villains. The message encountered here is one of disability associated with moral failing. Then if children are not proactively introduced to bodies with disabilities, what mental model are they experiencing and having reinforced? If we then combine that with early education, where lots of content about the world we live in is Eurocentric and predominantly focused on white culture and history – in the storybooks, the history, music and art, what schema-building about society is taking place? In essence, we have to question the baseline for children's social schema. It is the foundational learning upon which they will pin all future learning.

Why do We Teach What We Teach?

We can consider several layers of rationale behind the content that we choose to put in front of our young people.

Macro-Level

This is the level of influence over content that we may be least aware of, but permeates all of the other levels of influence on the curriculum (Figure 3.1). Bhambra et al. (2018: 5) point out that universities are the starting point for racist discourses, stating that 'in the

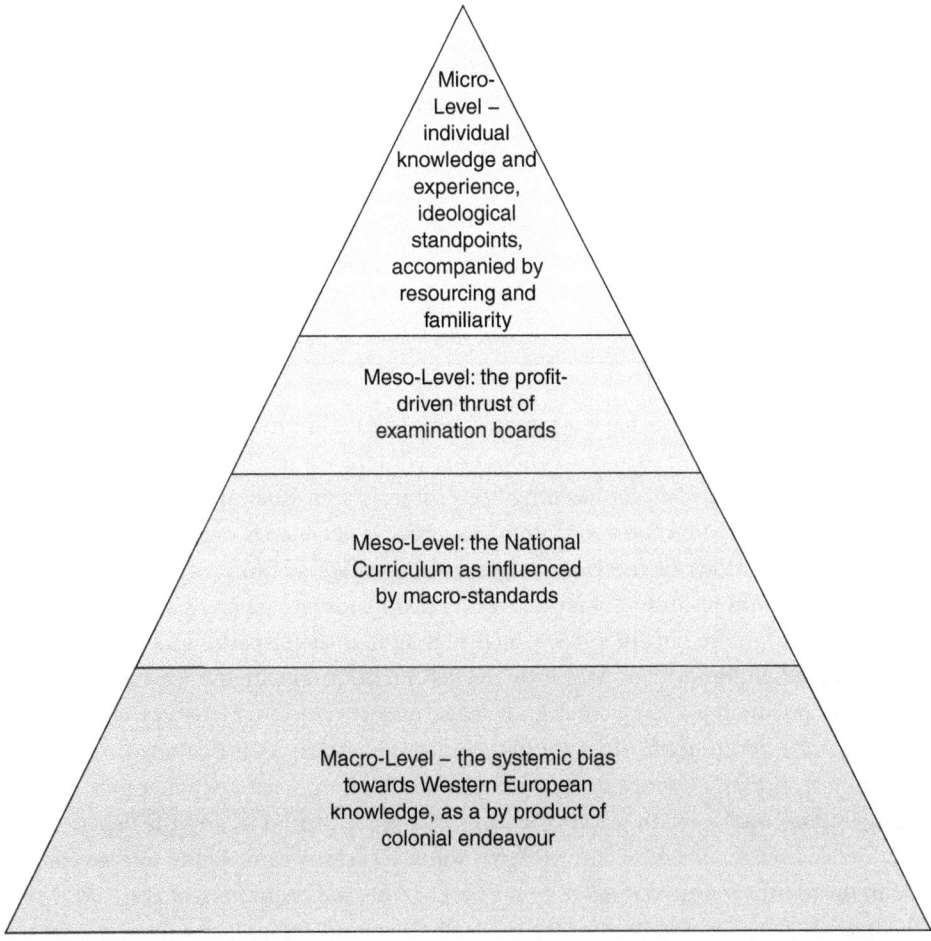

Figure 3.1 Influences on teaching content

colonial metropolis, universities provided would-be colonial administrators with knowledge of people they would rule over' and 'the foundation of European higher education institutions in colonised territories itself became an infrastructure of empire, an institution and actor through which the totalising logic of domination could be extended; European forms of knowledge were spread, local indigenous knowledge suppressed, and native informants trained'.

Reflecting on the work of Lander and Past (2002), we can see that Eurocentric models of thinking have influenced the content of the curriculum as it stands today (Table 3.1).

In turn, these macro-structures influence national policy on what is taught in schools.

Meso-Level

Maintained schools in the UK have to follow the National Curriculum, whereas Foundation schools have more freedom to deviate and Academies are not bound by the

Table 3.1 Models of Eurocentric thinking in the curriculum

Consideration	Potential impact on curriculum	References
Eurocentric models are based on binaries such as *reason* and *body*, *subject* and *object*, *culture* and *nature*, *masculine* and *feminine*	Racialised and heteronormative positionally of content; knowledge of male Western minds seen as superior	Berting (1993) Quijano (2000) Lander (2000b)
European history is universal	Western curriculum centres European narratives as it serves as a model from 'primitive to modern'	Dussel (2000) Quijano (2000)
European history is based on differentiating from 'others'	Non-European narratives are seen as backwards, inferior or 'savage'	Mignolo (1995) Quijano (2000)

National Curriculum, but have a responsibility to offer a broad and balanced curriculum. So, in theory, we are freer to choose the content we teach than ever before. And yet, the National Curriculum has long been subject to ideological influences, not least of which are centred on the viewpoints of successive Secretaries of State for Education.

The first iterations of the National Curriculum were as much engaged in debates about what would result in equipping young people for employment as anything else. Barring the Swann Report of 1985, which highlighted the disparity in achievement of 'West Indian' children, there was little explicit mention of catering for the needs of a diverse population via the actual knowledge imparted through the curriculum. The initial conversations about what should go into the National Curriculum are buried in the Subject Working Groups documentation and I would need a whole other book to analyse those! Fast forward to the Michael Gove years (2010–14), and the debate about knowledge itself – and whose knowledge is valuable – really came to the fore, as embodied in the Matthew Arnold reference: 'the best of what has been thought and said'. I find it interesting that the quotation, as used by Gove and his proponents – and in the National Curriculum 2013 – is truncated from: 'Culture being a pursuit of our total perfection by means of getting to know, on all the matters which most concern us, the best which has been thought and said *in the world*' (my own italics for emphasis). It is a shame that the whole quote was not included in the drive towards a knowledge-rich curriculum during those years and since.

There has been some shift towards diversity in the National Curriculum, and yet, references to what is taught remain vague. In the English curriculum, there is specific mention of 'seminal' world literatures, for example, but little directive to look at authorship from a range of author identities in order to foster critical perspectives. The lens narrows at Key Stage 4, where teachers are expected to teach students to 'read and appreciate the depth and power of the English literary heritage' through a series of recommended texts. In History, we are directed to the teaching of global civilisations such as the Indus Valley civilisations and Ancient Sumer at KS1 and KS2. At KS3, world histories are suggested, but with a narrower focus and the histories of Russia and the USA are recommended as options. In other subjects, such as Art, we see that there is a suggestion that students should be aware of 'great artists' but who this might entail is left to interpretation. In PE, there is no reference to knowledge related to the discipline outside of the procedural aspects of the subject, which, again, might lead to the omission of key diverse aspects of the curriculum.

Examination boards also play a role in what we choose to teach. I make no accusations here, but the profession has long battled between the need to provide a full, rounded education and to provide an education that meets the needs of the examination. Who decides what is examined? Well, in some cases, Michael Gove, who, in 2014, presided over examination reforms that included a greater focus on British history. In other cases, it is unclear, but the results are tangibly skewed towards male, white, Western European content. The Runnymede Trust found that only 'only 2.3 per cent of all named stand alone artists are from Black or South Asian backgrounds' in Art examination papers (Begum et al., 2024). In Music, only 4% of composers on the piano syllabus for the Associated Board of the Royal Schools of Music (ABRSM) examination were female composers. Teach First's report into diversity revealed that 'not a single woman's name explicitly features in the national curriculum for GCSE science. And in a sample analysis of the GCSE double science specifications from three of the major exam boards, we found that only two female scientists were explicitly named. In contrast, over 40 male scientists were mentioned, or had concepts or materials named after them' (Science and Technology Committee, n.d.).

It is clear that exam board content is not very diverse (although there has been a concerted shift in this circumstance of late). However, the sad truth is that curriculum content is far too constrained by the limitations of *our* own knowledge and experience. Exam boards have introduced new content that includes a range of diverse voices and examinable units and yet report annually that teachers stick to content that they know (and that is not diverse).

Micro-Level

In any given department there may be a desire to teach a broader range of ideas/texts/histories: but budget constraints may prevent the department from buying new resources, and time constraints may prevent them from being able to resource effectively content that is unfamiliar. It is heartening that exam boards are now providing more support when it comes to the design and delivery of examined content that is diverse and it must be noted that there has been a concerted effort to consult with a range of teachers from a range of backgrounds in order to be able to provide exam content that moves forward and broadens knowledge for students at Key Stage 4. It must also be argued that Key Stage 5 has always been at the vanguard of diverse content, particularly in the arts and humanities. The ability to choose the focus of your coursework path meant there is more scope for innovation in the subjects such as History and English Literature.

What does a department need in order to introduce a new unit of work? Teachers feel the need to develop their subject knowledge, to have a set of guiding resources, and an easily accessible set of exemplar materials in order to benchmark student progress. It might also be the case that teachers require more specific guidance on aspects of the new content that may be out of their experience. The simplest example of this is in delivering units of work on Jainism when this is something entirely unfamiliar compared to the content on Christianity or Islam. A teacher delivering content on this feels uncomfortable because they don't want to offend or get something wrong – which is an entirely understandable feeling.

There are tangible steps a school can take in order to facilitate significant shifts in curriculum content:

- Provide calendared time with a clear mandate to update subject knowledge, materials and resources, particularly if there are examination board changes.
- Provide ring-fenced budgets for specific subject knowledge development, such as funding for subject association membership.
- Encourage staff to attend subject-specific CPD (continuing professional development) focused on developing diverse knowledge.

How does Power Show up in Curriculum Content?

The work of Professor Michael Young on powerful knowledge has been seen as a clarion call for knowledge-rich curriculum design. Young advocates for a concept he describes as 'powerful knowledge', a concept that has been adopted by those who wish to see a more traditional curriculum in schools. The complexities of Young's arguments are often glossed over in less familiar circles; his work has been addressed by many academics in the field of education, but where he has been summarised, there are several misunderstandings of his work.

To start with, the term 'powerful knowledge' was meant to identify the structures within disciplines that create transcendent moments. Young states: powerful knowledge can 'enable students to acquire knowledge that takes them beyond their own experiences' (Young et al., 2014: 7) and that there are three distinct characteristics of powerful knowledge.

1   It is distinct from the 'common sense' knowledge we acquire through everyday life in that it allows students to 'transcend and liberate themselves' (Young, 2013: 118).
2   It is systematic in that it allows students to make cross-disciplinary connections.
3   It is specialised in that it has been formed by experts in the field.[1]

We might ask ourselves who would *not* want systematic, and specialised knowledge in our curriculum? One argument here is that these characteristics are based wholly in

---

[1]It is worth noting that the interpretations of this may be colonial in concept – who are the experts and how have we come to value them?

the realm of colonial discourse – making distinctions between personal and empirical and so on. When we start to interrogate the implications (not necessarily as imagined or intended by Professor Young) and look at the potential for misapplication we start to see that 'powerful knowledge' is just as susceptible to 'lethal mutations' as any other educational entity.

Firstly, Professor Young was originally clear in his distinction between 'powerful knowledge' and the 'knowledge of the powerful', as exemplified in his assertion that knowledge cannot be defined by the prevailing powers (www.tes.com, n.d.). Yet, in interpretation, the concept of powerful knowledge has been annexed into discourses about what kind of knowledge makes you socially mobile, perhaps more so than Young intended. The simple fact that the word 'power' exists in the phrase 'powerful knowledge', we are bound to its implications of who holds power, who we can be with it, and what we are without it.

Ford (2022) points out that the 'lethal mutation' lies in some schools aligning themselves with what Young called the 'Future-1' school, in which 'the main purpose of a Future-1 curriculum is to transmit a fixed canon of knowledge, believed to be somehow a-social, to enable students to maintain these social norms and structures into the future. It is the 'knowledge of the powerful'. In short, it is knowledge that is deemed valuable by white, Western European culture. It is no surprise, then, to see that Young's work was appropriated in the Gove years and formed a large influence on the curriculum reforms that took place at that time.

Another significant influence on the thinking around what we teach lies in the work of E.D. Hirsch. E.D. Hirsch is often deemed a culturally conservative commentator, when he himself believed that he was progressive, advocating through the concept of a common cultural literacy for social justice. But he failed to recognise the limitations of his own thinking: his projected common culture was firmly based in white culture, stemming from English art, history and literature. The inevitable implication of this centring of white American culture meant the omission of references to the culture, the history, the ideas and the literature of those who make up American society – at the time, as now, richly diverse.

In 2013, Michael Gove, quoting Gramsci, said: 'The accumulation of cultural capital – the acquisition of knowledge – is the key to social mobility.' Cultural capital, as a term used here, is heavily influenced by Hirsch's thinking and it reappears in many forms. In the Ofsted framework of 2019, we see it defined as 'the essential knowledge that pupils need to be educated citizens, introducing them to the best that has been thought and said and helping to engender an appreciation of human creativity and achievement' (Ofsted, 2019).

We come full circle. Theories of knowledge are imbued with narratives about power. The implications are troubling. Cultural capital is the best of what has been thought and said. The best of what has been thought and said belongs to one section of society. Your culture, your capital, your powerful knowledge is less valuable than ours. In this case, young people from all cultures and identities are expected to value, and learn, one culture's knowledge – to assimilate, in fact. While there is merit in understanding the culture one lives in, it is also important to recognise that culture is not the preserve of one group of people.

How do We Disrupt Power Structures in the Curriculum?

Christine Counsell is well known as an exponent of the concepts of 'core knowledge' and 'hinterland knowledge' in a curriculum. The idea of core knowledge, as Counsell herself has explained, is that it forms the basis of knowledge in that subject area (Counsell, 2018a). It is the knowledge that needs to be retained for future use. Hinterland knowledge is knowledge that enriches the core, it serves to illustrate, to enhance and to demonstrate core knowledge. The two aspects of Counsell's curriculum theory are not hierarchical, although it is acknowledged that an excess of hinterland knowledge can be a distraction from the core.

As teachers who want to create a diverse curriculum, we must ask questions about how schools implement the idea of core and hinterland into their curriculum. Is the decision about what is 'core' knowledge made by minds that are aware that knowledge itself is political and defined by our history of colonial activity? How do we decide what is the core content of a topic?

In *Epistemologies of the South*, Boaventura de Sousa Santos (2014) defines the filters that influence our decision making about what to teach our students. He explains that we have been conditioned to value knowledge that upholds three tenets of our society: colonisation/imperialism, capitalism and patriarchy. Therefore, our understanding of what is 'valued' knowledge is skewed by these filters. We teach what we have been con-ditioned to believe is important. Unfortunately for us, and our students, this often means that we place knowledge into categories or hierarchies. Going back to Counsell's concept of core and hinterland knowledge, it is all too common that educators, in the quest to diversify their curriculum, end up shifting diverse content into the hinterland of their subject and forgetting that core knowledge can be diverse too.

How would we apply this if we were teaching a textiles lesson on weaving?

In the left-hand part of Figure 3.2, we see that the core knowledge is British-centric and may lead to misconceptions about the topic of weaving. The 'diverse' knowledge is reserved for the hinterland, where it has a place, certainly; however, in the right-hand side of the figure, we see a subtle shift in narrative. The core knowledge here is about the origins of weaving and, arguably, is far more accurate as a starting point.

Counsell never intended for her concept to be interpreted as a hierarchy. How does this misapplication play out in a curriculum sequence? It is simple. On a macro level, units of work are centred on content that is predominantly white and Western European. They make up the 'taught' and 'instructible' material. Content that could be described as diverse then sits in the hinterland of the unit of work and worse – in the homework, in the self-directed project, in the wider reading.

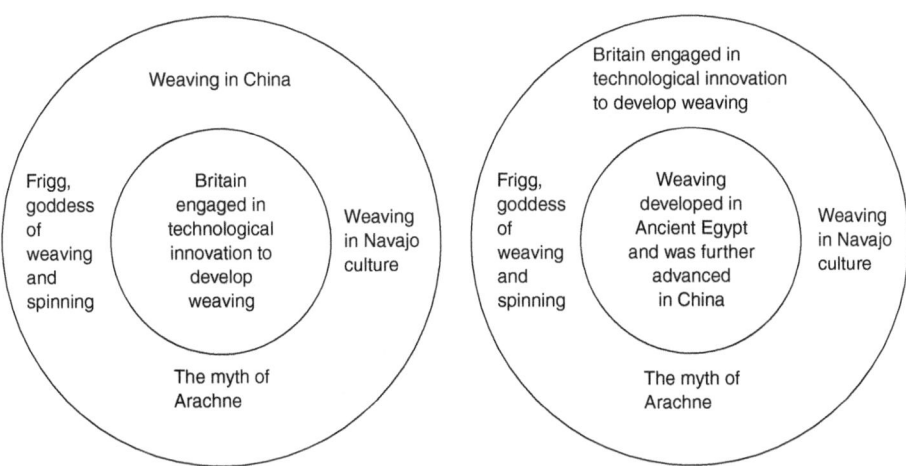

Figure 3.2 Decentring power in DT

In her groundbreaking work on the Haringey Education Partnership Humanities curriculum, Counsell demonstrates that her concepts of core and hinterland are not hierarchical and should not be used to relegate diverse material. In the curriculum she designed with Steve Mastin, Counsell foregrounds the history and cultures of South Asian and Middle Eastern people as part of the sequence of history. This content forms the 'core' of her curriculum because she recognises the importance of the Indus Valley civilisation to the development of global culture. She recognises the importance of Baghdad as a centre of commerce, culture and art in relationship to the development of European cities and cultures. At no point does Counsell start with British history, then slot in a unit of work containing this diverse content. She puts it front and centre of the curriculum and weaves towards the story of Britain from there. This is a useful disruption of Eurocentric thinking.

The key takeaway here is that there is a mistaken belief that the 'diverse' elements of the subject curriculum can be squeezed into the hinterland of the subject, as a form of supplementary knowledge that enriches. While there is certainly scope to include a much wider range of stories, examples and faces into the hinterland of a subject, it cannot be the only space in which the diverse exists. By doing so, we reinforce undesirable power structures – placing a white, Western European canon of knowledge at the centre of the galaxy of learning.

Counsell (2018b) also explains to us that disciplinary knowledge is a valuable tool to reflect on the 'ever-shifting now'. She outlines the importance of disciplinary questions that allow us to understand how knowledge is established – and of course, in doing so, we are invited to examine power, colonisation, patriarchy and other defining factors. How might the examination of knowledge in this way appear in different subjects? Table 3.2 gives two examples.

Table 3.2 Disciplinary questions in Science and Geography

Subject	Statement	Disciplinary questions
Science	To be able to validate observations, we need measurable data	How has this scientific thinking been formulated? Why are data valued? Can science exist without data reporting? Are there scientists who observe and report differently?
Geography	Mercator is the most important cartographer in the world	Why might Mercator be centred? Why are other cartographers seen as less important? How does geographical knowledge come to be formed?

Organising Knowledge

Sue Sanders, Professor Emeritus at the Harvey Milk Institute, coined the phrase 'usualising' to outline how LGBTQ+ teaching can be woven into daily interactions. She deliberately avoids the word 'normalising' as it carries negative and binary connotations. In an interview, Sanders recounts:

> So I had been talking for some time about a concept that I had been playing with, which was usualising. I felt the term normalising was problematic that we just could not reclaim it. There's certain terms you can't reclaim and I think saying that we're normal or normalising just has too many problematic connotations. So I came up with this term usualising and my concept was that you don't do the gay lesson. What you do is you usualise this throughout the curriculum. (Sanders, 2019)

The distinction that Sanders makes here is useful not just for LGBTQ+ identities, but all marginalised identities within the curriculum. Diversity is not therefore something to be held under a microscope, but something to be woven into the curriculum without further comment.

In practice, it means that standalone 'diversity' units are not helpful in curriculum design in terms of logic either.

If diversity is to be truly embedded and usualised in our curricula, it is important to consider how curriculum theory and design principles can be used to create useful, logical, well-sequenced and deep pathways of learning. Sequencing a curriculum effectively is the process of defining the narrative of your subject. This is a useful way of thinking about what is worthy of inclusion into the building blocks and the micro-elements of a curriculum – it tells a story to your students, the story develops in complexity, the story has a beginning and a present, the story is peopled with characters, the story has a meaning or a message.

When we decide to include diverse content, the most obvious error that is made is in the unconsidered insertion of new material simply because it is diverse. This tokenistic approach does not take into account the 'narrative' of the subject – it is done under the assumption that the content has to be there regardless of how it affects the coherence of the curriculum. Placing a unit of work called 'LGBTQ+ History' into the KS3 curriculum at the end of Year 9 because it is 'additional' or 'supplementary' work to fill time before the GCSE kicks in in Year 10 is not effective curriculum design. If the History curriculum up to that point is broadly chronological, then how does 'LGBT History' sit in that chronology? The potential message that students receive about the placement of this unit of work might be that LGBTQ+ History is a 20th- century module. Of course, if then the content of that module of work references a Stonewall-plus perspective, that assumption about LGBTQ+ people being a modern phenomenon may be reinforced.

It would seem more prudent to ensure that LGBTQ+ history is woven through the curriculum, if that is content that you deem useful and important for your students to know. To avoid students believing that poets of colour only write about conflict and oppression, it is important to view the whole of the poetry trajectory in the English curriculum, consider form over content and include poets of colour in units of work that are broader in scope than those of the old AQA Poetry Anthology. This avoids tokenism, and usualises the presence of these texts in the curriculum.

Planning Sequences

You may want to ask yourself some questions about how diverse content sits in the sequence of your curriculum:

1   How does this content relate to the chronology, or narrative of my subject?
2   How does it build effectively on the content that has come before it?
3   How will it serve as a basis for understanding of content that comes later?

These questions allow for better decisions about placement of diverse content in the curriculum. A poem by a writer of colour that echoes the themes of Romanticism might be placed in a unit of work on Romantic poetry to demonstrate the evolution of the genre, rather than a poem being placed in a standalone unit of work called 'Diverse Poetry'. If the aim is to demystify people who are 'Othered' by society, we do not want reinforce the 'Othering' by grouping writers by their race or culture.

It is important to note that diversifying the curriculum is not always about whole units of work. There are three levels that we can play with when considering how diverse content fits into the curriculum (Figure 3.3).

In some subjects, you might find that diverse content sits naturally into a whole unit of work. In others, you might find that diverse content is a component within a unit of work, and in some cases, it may be necessary to include diverse content in the 'did-you-know' moments of teaching.

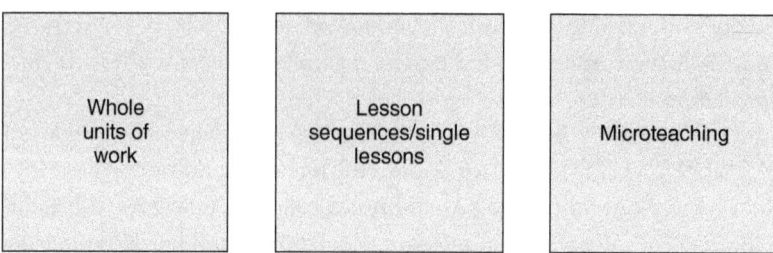

Figure 3.3 Three levels of diverse content

.... **REFLECTION QUESTIONS**

- How confident are you in articulating how power and knowledge are combined?
- Can you identify the influences on the knowledge you teach in your curriculum?
- How can you deliberately disrupt old patterns of knowledge and power through your curriculum content and sequencing?
- How can you usualise the presence of marginalised groups in your curriculum?
- What structures can you use to include diverse content meaningfully and logically?

....

4

DESIRABLE LENSES

Evaluation is key to ensuring the diverse curriculum is effective. We must ask ourselves questions about what is being taught already, and how, so that we can see gaps and patterns in the knowledge we are offering to children and young people. As much as the good old 'audit' has developed a reputation for being a pointless paper exercise, I am going to defend it when evaluating a curriculum. To be able to truly see what is in front of you in terms of content and narrative, there needs to be a process of investigation and reflection of the whole curriculum, and by the whole curriculum, I mean not just the academic content, but the wider curriculum mechanisms as well.

It is as good a place as any to use the Equality Act 2010 to begin the journey. Within the Act, in the form of the Protected Characteristics, we have an in-built and ready-made checklist for seeing the presence of marginalised groups, both in the academic curriculum and in the wider curriculum.

It might be the case that you want to apply a model of evaluative effectiveness as part of this process. Table 4.1 lists some aspects you might want to consider.

Table 4.1 Aspects of evaluation of the curriculum

Aspect to be evaluated	Questions
Current views of the curriculum	How do students receive the curriculum as it stands?
	What do they feel is missing?
Impact of the curriculum on outcomes	How does the current curriculum impact on outcomes? What prevents better outcomes?
Impact of the curriculum on pastoral matters	How does the curriculum cater for the pastoral needs of the students?
	What gaps exist in delivering the best pastoral care through the curriculum?

Applying a model for evaluation might support you in setting a direction in terms of what you are looking for in the curriculum itself. Sometimes, the curriculum can feel like a mammoth beast. How do you eat an elephant? One bite at a time.

Using the Protected Characteristics as a Guide to Evaluation

In this section, you will find a series of questions that can ask your teams about how the protected characteristics are made visible in the curriculum.

Age

In the curriculum, we may not immediately see how representation of age appears and how it might be relevant. Age is a characteristic that belongs to all of us in some way at different stages of our lives and how young people go about developing positive schema about ageing may be an opportunity in the curriculum. In her chapter as part of the book *Diverse Educators: A Manifesto*, entitled 'Storybook Villains: Where are the Positive Older Role Models in the English Literature Curriculum?', Savitri Patel states: 'Self image is a key determinant in our experience of aging' (Kara and Wilson, 2022: 50). It may be worth exploring how age, ageing and age-related health appears in a range of subjects as it is intrinsically linked to personal development and sense of self.

Another underrepresented area is that of menopause. The impact of menopause on the body has become more and more visible in society, with loud calls for teachers to have more training in this area. Professor Joyce Harper et al. (2022) surveyed women about their educational experiences of menopause and 90.2% stated they had not been educated about the menopause at all.

Academic Curriculum

- Where do you explore media bias against older women?
- How is menopause taught to young people?
- Where do students encounter legislation against age discrimination?
- How do different societies cater for an ageing population?
- How do we preserve the learning of the older generations?
- What is retirement and how does it work?

Wider Curriculum

- Where do students encounter the older generation or partake in intergenerational activities?
- How do students hear the voices of those who have retired from their careers?

Disability

According to the 2021 Census, 17.8% of people in England and Wales identified themselves as disabled. In real terms, that equates to 10.4 million people with disabilities. When we look at disability through different lenses – the non-visible, for example – we can see that there is a lot of learning needed. Students themselves will often find themselves labelled with a disability and will not always have the agency, or sense of self yet, to be able to consider their place in the world. This is certainly true of neurodiverse children. Where in the curriculum do we address the historical and contemporary issues associated with disability and allow our students to explore a nuanced representation of people with disabilities? How do we enable them to see themselves represented positively?

Academic Curriculum

- How do students learn about the language of disability?
- How do students learn about variance in disability – that it is not just a visible physical characteristic?
- How do students learn about accessibility, accessibility design and legislation related to accessibility?
- Where do young people read stories about people with disabilities that go beyond stereotypes?
- When do students encounter the problematic history of disability, including eugenics?
- Where in the curriculum do students have the opportunity to learn sign language?
- How do students explore neurodiversity?
- Where in the curriculum do students encounter significant figures with disabilities who have contributed to a particular field?
- Where are misconceptions about disability addressed?

Wider Curriculum

- Where do young people meet people with disabilities in a real-life context?
- How are students encouraged to share their own or family members' experiences of disability?
- What support groups are there for students with disabilities in your educational setting and how do they access them?

Gender Reassignment

Of the responses to the gender identity questions on the 2021 Census, 0.5% of the population stated that their gender identity was different from their gender assigned at birth. While this statistic is tiny compared to that of disabilities in the England and Wales, gender reassignment is a protected characteristic that requires careful handling in the curriculum. Statistics show that hate crimes against transgender people are high in prevalence, with the Home Office reporting that 'in 2020/2021, 2,630 Hate Crimes against transgender people were recorded by the Police, an increase of 16% from the previous year' (Stop Hate UK, 2021). The sad reality is that transgender people are at significant risk from harm. It is clear that violence against transgender people is facilitated by and exacerbated by social media. A recent collaborative report by Brandwatch and Ditch the Label revealed through analysis of 10 million online posts over a three-and-a-half year period 1.5 million transphobic comments amid the wider conversation around trans people (Brandwatch, 2019). The report makes for sobering reading.

Academic Curriculum

- How do students learn about transgender people in history?
- How do we explore how society creates gender identities?
- What do students learn about prominent transgender figures, such as athletes, and how is the conversation handled?
- How do we approach the topic through science?
- What stories are told about transgender experiences?
- How do students learn about hate crimes and prejudice against transgender people?
- How are pronouns dealt with in Modern Foreign Languages?
- How do we explore other cultures' perceptions of gender and sex?
- How do we explore the nuances of the debates around sports, single sex spaces and rights protections?

Wider Curriculum

- How do students encounter transgender people in real life?
- How are transgender students supported in connecting with each other (if wanted)?
- How do the families of transgender children connect and have a voice?

Maternity and Pregnancy

Apart from the obvious benefits of teaching young people about maternity and pregnancy, there are some important aspects of this protected characteristic that could appear in the curriculum. Pregnancy is often delivered (if you'll forgive the pun) through a biological lens, with the mechanics of it being the focus. Often, this is followed by the hazards of teenage pregnancy. The concepts of maternity and paternity are often left to be discovered when one reaches that stage of one's life. So where in our curriculum is there space to explore the issues surrounding pregnancy and maternity? Furthermore, there are huge misconceptions about adoption and fostering that could be addressed in the curriculum. There are more children in care than there ever have been, as of 2023 (explore-education-statistics.service.gov.uk, n.d.).

Academic Curriculum

- Where does the curriculum engage students in understanding beyond the biological processes of pregnancy?
- Where do students learn about the rights of parents generally and at work?
- How is fertility/infertility addressed in the curriculum?
- How do students learn about the impact of pregnancy on their bodies?
- Where do students come to understand the legislation and rights surrounding pregnancy, maternity and paternity?
- How do students explore the adoption process? How do they learn about adoption legalities and rights?
- How are common misconceptions around gender roles and parenting addressed (for example, 'mum is primary caregiver')?

Wider Curriculum

- How do students hear first hand about parenting experiences?
- How do adopted children/children in care connect with each other (if appropriate)?
- What networks and support groups are signposted for young parents?

Marriage and Civil Partnership

The landscape around marriage and civil partnership has changed considerably in the past two decades, so it should come as no surprise that there are misunderstandings and misconceptions about the state of play with this protected characteristic. Everything from marital rights, to who can marry and where, might be part of your curriculum. Civil partnerships became legal in the UK in December 2005 and the Marriage (Same Sex Couples) Act was passed in July 2013. The UK was by no means the first to legalise marriage between same-sex couples – that happened in the Netherlands in 2001. Ask yourself these questions as you evaluate your content:

Academic Curriculum

- Do young people understand their rights when it comes to marriage, for example, at what age you can get married?
- Does your curriculum reference the idea of consent to marriage?
- How does your curriculum define marriage and civil partnership, considering the religious and legal aspects of those terms?
- At what point do students understand that same-sex couples can be married if the laws of a country allow for this?

- What do students learn about civil partnership and legal rights?
- How do students explore the idea of divorce, including legal aspects of the process?
- Where are students made aware that they cannot be discriminated against on the basis of their marital status?

Wider Curriculum

- How do the voices of those in civil partnerships/LGBT marriages get shared in the pastoral structures of the school?
- Do students see the school celebrating marriages and civil partnerships of all staff, not just heterosexual couples?

Race

It would appear to some that looking at race as a protected characteristic is the simplest of evaluative tools. In one way, that is entirely true, in that you could determine the presence of global majority groups in the curriculum. In another sense, evaluating your curriculum with race in mind is one of the most complex processes you can go through. Race is not a single identity; it is not the same as ethnicity, and it often differs culturally and geographically. What is clear though is the need to create a representative, interrogating and anti-racist curriculum that brings decolonisation into the equation. You might want to ask these questions, by no means exclusive, during evaluation:

Academic Curriculum

- What is the racial balance of the curriculum?
- How is anti-Black racism addressed?
- What are the gaps in racial presence in the curriculum?
- If there is presence of different racial groups, what is the balance between positive representation and histories of marginalisation?
- How do other global majority groups, such as South Asian, or East Asian, fare in your curriculum?
- Is there a recognition of the impact of colonisation in the curriculum?

Wider Curriculum

- What affinity groups exist for ethnic groups in school that aren't just related to attainment and progress?
- How does the school celebrate race and culture more widely?
- How are students encouraged to talk about their own racial experiences?
- How do trips and visits reference racial histories?

Religion and Belief

In the 2021 Census, the religion question sparked furious debate about the nature of religion in England and Wales. The Census states: 'For the first time in a census of England and Wales, less than half of the population (46.2%, 27.5 million people) described themselves as "Christian", a 13.1 percentage point decrease from 59.3% (33.3 million) in 2011' and that '"No religion" was the second most common response, increasing by 12.0 percentage points to 37.2% (22.2 million) from 25.2% (14.1 million) in 2011' (Office for National Statistics, 2021). There is clearly a shifting landscape when it comes to religion itself, and we may need to consider what that looks like in the curriculum. Religion and belief show up in the curriculum in fairly obvious ways. We study Religious Education in a variety of forms, regardless of the country in which we live. Sometimes, this is pluralistic and even handed, sometimes it is mono-religious according to the laws and guidance of the state. Wherever you are and however religion appears in your curriculum, you can ask yourself these questions:

Academic Curriculum

- Which religions are seen as 'important' and which religions are not seen as such?
- How do religions that have faced persecution show up in your curriculum?
- Is there space for discussion of beliefs without impinging on the rights of another protected characteristic?
- Is there space for discussion about non-belief/atheism?
- How do we teach about Humanism?
- How does the wider curriculum (plays, celebrations and so on) attach itself to religion and if it does, which one?
- How does the study of religion reflect the needs (and the possible lack of knowledge) of a local community?

Wider Curriculum

- Who is invited to share aspects of their religion across all religious denominations?
- How do students engage in religious practice (if desired) in school?
- How does 'collective worship' acknowledge all religions?

Sex

Sex is determined as your biological sex at birth. This is a complex and often controversial area, and we have seen many arguments on social media and in the mainstream press about how to define sex as opposed to gender. One way we can assess our curriculum in terms of sex is in the way we manage the presence and balance of male and female persons in the curriculum. It may also be worth looking at how we teach about biological sex. It is important to note, again, the need to take a 'fair and dispassionate' approach, which may mean presenting nuance in a way that has not been presented before, especially when considering the needs of our young transgender students.

Academic Curriculum

- How is biological sex taught in school?
- Is there an exploration of the scientific viewpoints on the intricate web of biological sex and gender?
- Is there an attempt to affirm the presence of transgender and non-binary young people?
- Is there room for discussion on women's rights and roles in the society?
- Is there a balance where possible between male and female significant figures in the curriculum?

Wider Curriculum

- Can students discuss gendered spaces in school sensitively?
- How do events like Sports Day work in terms of sporting choice?

Sexual Orientation

In the UK context, the repeal of Section 28 in 2003 means that educators are now able to discuss sexual orientation in the curriculum. It is evident that discussing sexuality is still not seen as legal in some places. If you are legally and culturally able to discuss sexuality in your context, then you may want to consider the following:

Academic Curriculum

- Is there a recognition of different types of families, including same-sex parents and extended family members?
- Does your curriculum make young people aware of the global differences in approaches to sexuality in an age-appropriate fashion?
- Does the RSE curriculum include age-appropriate references to LBGTQ+ people?
- Does the PSHE curriculum allow space for discussion about LGBTQ+ history?
- Are the LGBTQ+ significant figures in the curriculum both historical and contemporary?
- Do the significant LGBTQ+ figures have agency and have they advocated for themselves successfully?

Wider Curriculum

- When do students meet people of different sexual orientations and hear their experiences?

- How do clubs and groups function in school for LGBTQ+ students?
- How do LGBTQ+ families engage in school life?
- How does the school signpost pastoral support for LBGTQ+ students and their families?

....**REFLECTION QUESTIONS**

- What aspects of your curriculum need evaluating?
- How do you know what is working and what is not working?
- What questions do you need to ask of students, staff, families and the community?
- How can you use the Equality Act to support you in your evaluative process?
- How will you report these findings?
- What are the clear and actionable steps to ensure there is meaningful change?

....

5

COMMON TRAPS

Being aware of how your current curriculum might create problematic narratives is essential. Being able to pattern spot means that we can eliminate perception errors about people, places and ideas over time.

Patriarchy

In 1982, Dale Spender wrote: 'What is considered inherently interesting is knowledge about men. Because men control the records, and the value system, it is generally believed that it is men who have done all the exciting things, it is men who have made (his) tory, made discoveries, made inventions and performed feats of skill and courage – according to men. These are the important activities and only men can engage in them, so we are led to believe. And so it is that the activities of men become the curriculum' (Spender, 1982: 58).

Is it true that men *are* the curriculum? The National Curriculum (Primary and Secondary) as of 2023 does not name many historical figures in relation to the varying subjects, but when it does, the balance of men and women named pans out as shown in Table 5.1.

The list is, as expected, predominantly male. Three out of the ten women named as suggestions are nurses. Only two out of the 34 people named are of colour. What is interesting is how much schools supplement the inclusion of named people in the curriculum, and how male-dominated the curriculum stays under the curation of us as teachers – products of our own education in many ways.

Recognising reasons why the curriculum might be male-dominated rests in three strands of possibility. Firstly, we know that women were excluded from many spheres of public life, resulting in a lack of visibility in the historical record. It is not hard to see then how women are not seen as contributors to the field of knowledge across subjects. Secondly, we are aware that historical perspectives have favoured male narratives in science, exploration and politics, thereby excluding narratives of women in these fields. Lastly, public recognition for achievement has centred on men historically, so women have been relegated to the lower echelons of historical endeavour.

Table 5.1 Named figures in the curriculum by gender

Men	Women
John Dunlop	Jane Goodall
Charles Mackintosh	Ruth Benerito
John McAdam	Mary Anning
David Attenborough	Elizabeth I
Spencer Silver	**Rosa Parks**
Galileo Galilei	Emily Davison
Isaac Newton	**Mary Seacole**
Carl Linnaeus	Florence Nightingale
Charles Darwin	Edith Cavell
Alfred Wallace	Rosalind Franklin
Christopher Columbus	
Neil Armstrong	
William Caxton	
Tim Berners-Lee	
Pieter Bruegel the Elder	
L.S. Lowry	
William Shakespeare	
Pythagoras	
Watson, Crick and Wilkins	
John Dalton	
Robert Hooke	
Henry VII	
Cromwell	
Charles Darwin (again)	

As a common trap in the curriculum, a patriarchal perspective is evident in most subjects. It is hard to unravel the systemic bias towards men in our curriculum; however, it is not impossible. It takes thought and resources, and crucially, an understanding that making space for women in the curriculum 'is not about slotting women into a pre-existing framework. It is about reconstructing history as we know it. Women's history challenges, untidies, disorganises and unravels the well-knit narrative of men's ideas and activities' (Bourdillon and Bartley, 1988: 10).

Encounter Hierarchy

Natalie Johnston, a Trust-Wide Subject Lead for Science, defines 'encounter hierarchy' as the effect through which we allocate importance to a knowledge according to the sequence in which that knowledge is 'met' in the curriculum. Consider what is centred in your curriculum: what do students 'meet' first? This is exemplified in Science in the teaching of biology. The first time that students encounter photosynthesis, it may be through practical work in which oxygen is collected. This leads to students' misunderstanding that the purpose of photosynthesis is production of oxygen rather than glucose. This misconception can take years to unpick because teachers do not recognise where it may have been embedded. Now applying this to, say, a Computer Science curriculum, it may be the case that students learn about the development of computing through the work of Charles Babbage first and *then* learn of Ada Lovelace's importance in the development of computing. She is not centred.

This concept applies in other subjects too. If the artists children 'meet' first are all male and white, and then there is a move to introducing women and people of colour afterwards, what is the message young people receive about their order of importance or their value in society's eyes? If students only ever see men centred first in Religion, Geography, Drama, English Literature and so on, what are they learning? Potentially that women are footnotes with very little contribution to any field. Women as an afterthought is just as damaging as not seeing any women at all.

It rests with the teaching profession to make decisions about how to consciously craft the curriculum to ensure that we meet the women, where possible, who have been sidelined historically first, rather than as additions on STEM days on Black female scientists, or as part of units of work that perpetuate the idea of women as 'Other', such as in units of work on Women in Literature.

It goes without saying that in encounter hierarchy, those with marginalised identities are pushed further down the list.

What is the order of visibility of these people and, perhaps, their perceived value in the curriculum?

- White, straight, able-bodied men?
- White, straight, able-bodied women?
- Global majority women?
- Global majority, able-bodied women?
- White, straight men with disabilities?
- Global majority lesbians?
- Global majority gay men?
- White gay men?
- White gay women?

Heteronormativity

Heteronormativity is the assumption that the default or correct sexual orientation is straight. It centres the idea that 'normal' relationships exist only between a man and a woman and that anything outside of these norms is considered abnormal or inferior.

The work of Adrienne Rich and Gayle Rubin helped to define heteronormativity. Michael Warner in 1991 then went on to popularise the term as part of emerging Queer Theory.[1] We live in a heteronormative culture. In our curriculum it means that we can be guilty of centring heterosexual identities and experiences because that is seen as the default relationship structure we are used to.

The 1980s saw a change in fledgling liberal attitudes towards sexuality. In 1983, a book called *Jenny Lives with Eric and Martin* hit the shelves of a library in South London. It wasn't until 1986 that there was a public outcry over its presence, but this outcry led to Lord Halsbury tabling a Private Member's Bill called 'An Act to Refrain Local Authorities from Promoting Homosexuality'. In 1988, this bill was enacted and became Section 28. This legislation stated that local authorities 'shall not intentionally promote homosexuality or publish material with the intention of promoting homosexuality' or 'promote the teaching in any maintained school of the acceptability of homosexuality as a pretended family relationship' (Local Government Act, 1988).

The impact of Section 28 on the curriculum cannot be underestimated. Any reference to homosexuality was expunged. LGBTQ+ was erased from the curriculum. The threat of losing your teaching job if you did 'promote' homosexuality meant that it was too risky to mention. The legacy of Section 28 is drawn on in several books that explore how teachers lived under this threat. In *Pretended: Schools and Section 28: Historical, Cultural and Personal Perspectives*, Dr Catherine Lee (2023) outlines the terror and danger for LGBT teachers teaching under Section 28. Paul Baker's *Outrageous! The Story of Section 28 and Britain's Battle for LGBT Education* draws on narratives from the LBGTQ+ community and looks closely at the legacy of Section 28 (Baker, 2023).

The National Curriculum was conceived in 1988 and so was Section 28. It is no coincidence then that the original iteration of the curriculum was entirely free from references to sexuality other than the heteronormative stance. While there have been changes, the legacy of Section 28 still exists in the reluctance to truly address the nuances of human sexuality as we understand them today, or as they were understood in the past.

This means we still see a reluctance to explore LGBTQ+ experiences during the Holocaust, or to include same-sex family representation in maths problems, and question whether we should include same-sex relationships, or transgender identities in the literature that we share with young people. It means that we centre heterosexual narratives over all others.

As Section 28 was not repealed until 2003 – incidentally, the year I started teaching – many teachers today still struggle to know how to teach about LGBT identities in the curriculum. As a result, the curriculum is still centred on heteronormativity.

In depictions of family life, we are drawn to the path of least resistance, drawing images of families that are two parent, male/female. In this, there is also a lack of

---

[1]I have deliberately changed the order in which these theorists have been recorded. This is an example of disrupting encounter hierarchies in terms of gender.

recognition that families come in all shapes and sizes. Heteronormativity manifests in the following ways in the curriculum:

- References to sexuality and relationships are almost exclusively heterosexual.
- There is an assumption of heterosexuality in all people mentioned in the curriculum.
- Relationships education centres on heterosexuality.
- Conversations around consent are centred around heterosexuality.
- Gender is binary and fixed.
- Families are centred on and assumed to be heterosexual structures.

The irony in all of this is that our young people live in a world where LGBTQ+ identities are usual. They have questions about LGBTQ+ life and relationships, they have family members in same-sex relationships and some know of non-binary and transgender people, and may even identify as non-binary or transgender themselves. So when we teach from a heteronormative position, we often forget to include conversations around consent from the perspective of LGBTQ+ people; we present gender as binary and fixed and fail to represent gender diversity and sexuality in family life.

The impact is clear. Young LGBTQ+ people do not see themselves represented, nor do they see any challenge to heteronormative thinking in the curriculum as often as they could. This may, of course, be related to fear of backlash from parents/carers, or the wider community.

Lack of Representation of the Global South

Obrillant Damus, in an article prepared for the International Commission on the Futures of Education (UNESCO), states: 'The products of Western and Western-centric education systems generally view the poor lacking in revenue in the global North and global South as also lacking in thought' (Damus, 2021). This worldview centres the northern hemisphere as the originator and perpetuator of knowledge and knowledge systems, also known as epistemologies. The history of epistemological development is complex, and it would be foolish to try and detail it here; however, an overview is possible.

European centred thinking, and adjacent to this, northern hemisphere thinking, has been privileged over time. It has been believed that northern hemisphere thinkers have shaped knowledge, recorded it and transmitted it; therefore, it must be more important and more valuable that southern hemisphere knowledge.

The work of Raewyn Connell helps us to understand the lack of representation of the Global South in the curriculum. She poses an interpretation of Metropole theory in which she explains the facets behind a dominant, northern hemisphere-centred epistemology. In it, she claims that the Global North is able to claim the centre of epistemological thought because it proposes that northern hemisphere knowledge is tacitly universal; she also references the belief that there is a timelessness to Global North knowledge; she links this to gestures of exclusion, such as reading lists that are predominantly or exclusively northern hemisphere based and finally, she points out that the Global North participates in a grand erasure, with the assumption that the Global South is an empty arena, a *terra nullius* (Connell, 2007).

What does this mean in our curriculum? It means that indigenous knowledge is dismissed; it means that knowledge originating in Australia, Southern Africa and South America is not valued by our education system. Beneath this is the belief that knowledge that has not been wheeled through academic structures such as the university is somehow not legitimate. So our students learn about a narrower range of thinkers, learn about the accomplishments of the Global North and fail to learn about thinking that might not be empirical in nature. If western (and thereby northern hemisphere) knowledge tends to be text-based, reductionist, hierarchical and dependent on categorisation, southern knowledge is seen as imprecise and intuitive, harder to capture, and based on millennia of experience.

Indigenous Knowledge Erased

Young people might learn about the work of Mark Bonta and Robert Gosford, in which they observe kites and falcons intentionally spreading fire using burning sticks to unburned land in order to harvest the insects that flee from the burning zones, but they might not learn this is common indigenous knowledge from northern Australia. The Alawa people have such a profound knowledge of these 'firehawks' that they are included in their creation stories.

Historical examples of cultivation of biodiversity exist in the southern hemisphere, but the scientific community, and therefore, the science curriculum, rarely look at these examples. Research shows that the Maya had an extraordinary approach to cultivating biodiverse gardens around villagers' houses. Anabel Ford of the Mesoamerican Research Center at the University of California at Santa Barbara details the skill and sophistication of these 'forest gardeners' (Ford and Nigh, 2016).

In the English KS3 Geography curriculum, we are asked to teach young people to 'understand how human and physical processes interact to influence and change landscapes, environments and the climate; and how human activity relies on the effective functioning of natural systems'. In the Scottish curriculum, we see a broader scope for inclusion of indigenous knowledge, where sustainability can be woven into the topics on people, place and the environment. There are similar opportunities in the Welsh and Northern Irish curricula, where indigenous peoples' interaction with the planet could be explored, such as the Shieling system and transhumance, both associated with agricultural practices of Scots Gaelic people (Mike, 2023). There is much to be learned and much to be admired in the way that indigenous populations connect with the Earth's natural resources and ensure that they are sustained. In fact, Raewyn Connell goes on to point out that 'the only possible future for social science on a world scale involves a principle of unification'(2007: 223); and in connecting 'different formations of knowledge in the periphery with each other' (2007: 213) and with knowledge from the metropole.

Gypsy Roma and Traveller Existence and Heritage Erased

Romany Gypsy, Roma and Irish Traveller communities face significant discrimination in our society. In *Findings from the Evidence for Equality National Survey*, data showed that:

- 62% of Gypsies and Travellers had experienced racial abuse, which was the highest out of all minority ethnic groups surveyed;
- 47% of Roma people had been racially assaulted; and
- 37% of Roma people have been physically attacked (Finney et al., 2023: 54–77).

The experiences of Gypsy, Roma and Traveller young people are laid bare in *Gypsy, Roma and Traveller Experiences in Secondary Education: Issues, Barriers and Recommendations* by The Traveller Movement. In this revealing text, The Traveller Movement cites government statistics that indicate the disproportionately high number of school exclusions. Their research also showed that Gypsy, Roma and Traveller children had experienced race-based bullying. We must also reflect on the lack of distinction between these communities as the terms are often used interchangeably, ignoring the rich and complex structures and cultures surrounding them. The erasure of sub-groups within the category proves problematic too: there is little understanding of itinerant fairground operators, for example, as cultural identity within the traveller community, or Scottish Travellers as opposed to Irish Travellers (The Traveller Movement, 2020).

The current curriculum does not explicitly mention the need for Gypsy, Roma and Traveller history and culture in the curriculum; in fact, the few references to this community are often found in brief references to the Roma people eradicated in the Holocaust, without any detailed exploration of the actual experiences of Roma people, or even a reference to the Romani names for what happened. The Traveller Movement recommendations include:

- Enhancing a sense of belonging through inclusion in the curriculum, beyond that of stereotypes.
- Using the history of Gypsy, Roma and Traveller communities to dispel myths that surround them.
- Educating teachers and providing them with materials that allow them to teach about Gypsy, Roma and Traveller culture without defaulting to media representations that can be hugely damaging.

To add, there is a wealth of opportunity to do this in several subjects. You might teach about Romani folk music in Music, looking at the five main components of Romani music. It might be the case that you look at the ways in which Romani culture has influenced other modes of art – such as flamenco, folk violin and fairground/circus performance. Or even look at Romani artists such as Otto Mueller or Gabi Jiménez. You might explore the role of fairs in British culture as part of the History curriculum. You might look at Romani literature using resources produced by the Council of Europe (Wogg, n.d.). You might want to explore art by Irish Travellers, or depictions of Irish Travellers in art over time.

Ableism and Erasure of Disability

I have little recollection of being taught about disability, other than the fact that people with disabilities exist and there are words we should not use about them. I could not have told you the word for discrimination against people with disabilities until I was much older. Not having a name for it meant I did not comprehend its impact. So what is ableism and how does it manifest in the curriculum?

According to Rauscher and McClintock (1997: 198), ableism can be defined as 'a pervasive system of discrimination and exclusion that oppressed people who have mental, emotional and physical disabilities'. In the curriculum, that might mean perpetuating stereotypes about people with disabilities and presenting disability as an undesirable state with associations with moral iniquity.

It is clear that there is a mandate to discuss disability in schools. The curriculum allows teachers to explore disability definitions, rights and advocacy through PSHE. There are opportunities to explore disability in Science, in Literature, in Sport and so on. But the curriculum does not address fundamental concepts in disability studies that might allow for a shift in perception of disability. Baglieri and Lalvani (2020), drawing on the work of Bamberg and Andrews (2004), describe the way in which 'master narratives' seek to 'Other' disability: 'Master narratives are culturally derived, taken-for-granted "knowledge," or dominant assumptions about what is considered normal or desirable in society (Bamberg and Andrews, 2004). Master narratives on disability characterize disability as something to be cured, eliminated, fixed, or overcome, and depict life with a disability as tragic, pitiable, and burdensome' (Baglieri and Lalvani, 2020: 2).

In the choices we make about Literature curriculum, we can see that disability narratives are predominantly designed to evoke pity. In teaching *A Christmas Carol*, we are struck by the character of Tiny Tim in all of his helplessness. It's not just the representation of Tiny Tim. In another common text, Steinbeck's *Of Mice and Men*, we have Lennie with his learning disability being associated with his inadvertent violence, and even one-handed Candy – a downtrodden, and occasionally mean-spirited side character. To go a step further, we might look Stevenson's *The Strange Case of Dr Jekyll and Mr Hyde*. In this extract about Hyde, we can see the association of physical 'deformity', disgust and fear of criminality. Hyde is an example of someone Martha Stoddard Holmes designates as having 'unspecified disabilities' in *Fictions of Affliction* (Holmes, 2004: 12.)

He is not easy to describe. There is something wrong with his appearance; something displeasing, something downright detestable. I never saw a man I so disliked, and yet I scarce know why. He must be deformed somewhere; he gives a strong feeling of deformity, although I couldn't specify the point. He's an extraordinary looking man, and yet I really can name nothing out of the way. No, sir; I can make no hand of it; I can't describe him. And it's not want of memory; for I declare I can see him this moment.

Students may study all of these texts in the course of their secondary education. The risk is the pattern, or overarching narrative, that is created not by just experiencing one of these negative representations, but a series of them, working to devalue over time people with disabilities.

One example of ableist teaching embedded in the curriculum, the exam specifications and therefore in the curriculum generally relates to what makes us human. It is taught that humans have 23 pairs of chromosomes. Emma Swift and Natalie Johnston, Trust-Wide Subject Leads for Science, recount a moment in teaching when a student asked this question: 'humans have 23 pairs of chromosomes, does that mean people with Down syndrome are not human?' The question left them reeling. What misconception was being created about disability and genetics here? How did the curriculum reinforce it? How many times had students seen the phrase '*humans* have 23 pairs of chromosomes'?

Not addressing cultural and social ableism in the curriculum leads to stereotyping, assumptions and exclusion. We might see this in PE when we emphasise what humans should be able to do with their bodies, emphasising a norm based on an able-bodied person. It might mean only focusing on Paralympians as the pinnacle of what a person with a disability might achieve. What message is being transmitted about how people with disabilities become valued?

It is also worth noting here that, often, people with disabilities are *spoken about* in schools, and yet we do not often hear their voices centred in the teaching. One of the common pitfalls of a curriculum that does not adequately address disability is in its erasure of disabled voices, as well as bodies. Where do students hear first-hand experiences of people with disabilities? Are there texts that can counter the negative portrayals of disability in what is considered canonical literature? We may need to look to contemporary texts to see a shift in portrayals, which means considering how to make space for them in our curriculum.

Victim Narratives

I alluded to this trap at the start of this book, but I want to spend some time considering how framing people's experiences *entirely* through the lens of oppression might be problematic long term.

It is first important to state that I am not advocating here for an erasure of oppression narratives. Young people need to learn about the Holocaust, about enslavement, about colonisation, about climate injustice and its effects, about famine and discrimination. The function of learning about oppression might be to recognise the difference between humanisation and de-humanisation. Freire (1970) tells us: 'And as an individual perceives the extent of dehumanization, he or she may ask if humanization is a viable possibility' (p. 43). We may also need to spotlight oppression to show that it is not a fixed point in history, but continues to generate oppressive realities for generations afterwards. In essence, we learn about oppressive pasts to avoid oppressive futures.

However, if we only locate people's experiences in oppression, we may be erasing examples of agency, creativity, flourishing and, indeed, power. Women, therefore, remain in the kitchen with no identity outside of their domestic spheres, Black history is confined to enslavement and colonisation, the history of LGBT+ people sits in legal and social condemnation. There is nothing else. In an article in the *Harvard Gazette*, we hear that according to 'Wellesley College Professor Cord J. Whitaker, "one of the most insidious and nefarious legacies of slavery and racism" is that Black people "are routinely led to believe that they have no history beyond chattel slavery in the Americas"' (Milano, 2021).

We can extend this concept to other identities who have faced oppression. Do those subjugated by the British Empire have no history beyond that of colonisation? Do those oppressed by legislation on sexuality have no history beyond that of criminalisation? The answer, of course, is no. There is more to the history of marginalised groups than their marginalisation.

What creates a sense of agency for a particular identity? I am drawn to the definition of agency from the Gender Equality Toolbox (part of the Bill and Melinda Gates Foundation). In this, agency is defined as a combination of decision making, collective action and leadership (Gender Equality Toolbox, n.d.). So how do we show that oppressed groups also made decisions, engaged in collective action and experienced leadership?

We might go a step further and also look to find positive representations of global cultures, LGBT+ people, people with disabilities, those of particular religions and so on. What about the art, music, design and innovation of those people? What about their histories of positive contribution and success? What about stories from outside of Western Europe and the colonial lens? In Ancient Mesopotamian mythology, disability is said to be a result of a war of words between Enki and Ninmah. Ninmah creates disability to show that there will be humans who cannot serve the gods she is fighting and Enki subverts her power by granting those with disabilities good lives. A story not often told in the western curriculum, perhaps.

The endpoint is clear. There is a child sitting somewhere in your classroom who needs to hear that they (whatever their identity might be) have a richer history that that of oppression. They have songs, paintings, sculptures, religions, languages and theatre, they have kingdoms, cultures and civilisations. Their bodies have been valued. Their gender is acknowledged.

··· **REFLECTION QUESTIONS**

- How many of these common traps appear in your curriculum?
- What is the balance of diversity across the curriculum? If you've worked to alleviate the patriarchal nature of the curriculum, what's next?
- How do we balance the narrative of oppression with narratives of agency?

···

6

ADAPTING THE CURRICULUM – A SCHOOL WIDE JOURNEY

The move towards diversity in the curriculum is an organisational responsibility and no matter what our role in that organisation, we have the opportunity to use our spheres of influence.

I work with schools and multi-academy trusts who are looking to diversify their curriculum. I am always struck by the whole-organisation commitment made to this process, and reminded regularly that considering DEI in schools is not the role of one person, but of many people combined.

The simple fact is that this work cannot be done alone. When an organisation wants to see a culture shift, a sure indicator of eventual failure is when the work is being done by individuals alone. All too often diversity, equity and inclusion work is championed by those with protected characteristics, so curriculum adaptations become piecemeal rather than strategic and embedded. It is not effective to expect curriculum change solely to be enacted by those who are gay or disabled, for example. While they might have some level of expertise in some curriculum content related to sexuality or disability, this work is effective when done by organisations and teams who have a vested interest in social justice overall.

The team makes the commitment and individuals take on the responsibility to uphold the school's commitment by developing their awareness, their subject knowledge and their expertise in delivering diverse content.

Becoming 'Literate' in Diversities

One of the easiest commitments we can make as we start the journey towards adapting the curriculum is to develop our own literacies when it comes to the protected characteristics.

More often than not, we are encouraged to become racially literate. However, race is not an individual issue divorced from other protected characteristics; therefore, if we are going to become racially literate we must also become literate in the language of sexuality, gender and ability (and so on) in order to provide the most effective curriculum content. If we remain unaware of the common traps that we as a society fall into when thinking about protected characteristics or indeed not thinking about protected characteristics in the curriculum then we cannot adapt the curriculum effectively.

How do we go about becoming more literate when it comes to the issues surrounding specific protected characteristics?

- Consume widely the literature, blogs, podcasts and articles on the protected characteristics.
- Connect with others who are engaged in the work on DEI, such as the Diverse Educators community (www.diverseeducators.co.uk; see Resources and Support).
- Reflect personally on your own biases, and how they were formed (and how are they sustained).
- Listen to lived experience: once you have read and spoken to those with lived experience and those who have done the research, the responsibility lies with you to recognise the assumptions you have made consciously or unconsciously over the years about particular groups of people.
- As Luvvie Ajayi says in her brilliant TED Talk: 'get comfortable with being uncomfortable' (2018). Discomfort is a useful tool in change movements. Discomfort provides a rationale and a motivation for change; and when we consider the adaptation of the curriculum we can use that discomfort to recognise where we need to learn and grow. Organisational change doesn't happen when comfort is the status quo.
- Try not to centre yourself in the discourse. As Emily Torres (2020) writes: 'Centering ourselves means that instead of truly listening to someone's experience, we derail or challenge the conversation by sharing our own. This harmful refocusing is always unsolicited and is an attempt to protect our privilege and make ourselves feel comfortable.'

Leading Organisational Change

Like with any other school initiative, we need to pay close attention to the way in which we institute organisational change. It is important to become familiar with change models so that there is move toward a sustainable change in the curriculum, one that hopefully outlives you in your post.

There are many change theorists to choose from, but the good news is that most follow a similar broad macro-trajectory, with small differences at the micro-trajectory level. I am most familiar with the change theory as delineated by Dr John Kotter in his eight-step model, as put forward in his much-lauded book, *Leading Change* (Kotter, 1996).

How one might adopt this model to implement and sustain change is shown in Table 6.1.

Table 6.1 Kotter's change model and relevant questions

Change step	Questions
Create urgency	How can we let people know this work is important? What is the persuasive element here? How do we ensure people know it matters?
Form a powerful coalition	Who are your early adopters? Who has the expertise and will to help? Who has influence that could drive this forward?
Create a vision for change	What does the change look like? What is the big picture for all of us? What will look and feel different as a result?
Communicate the vision	How can we share this vision without it being a slogan? What do people need to hear and focus on? Where will it exist? Whose voices need to be heard?
Empower action	How can we facilitate change? What space/time needs to be given to this change? How can we provide a sense of autonomy whilst sticking to our values?
Create quick wins	What will create momentum? What will keep people from flagging along the way? How will we celebrate the quick wins?
Build on the change	How do we add depth to the change? How will we commit to ongoing conversation? What will be our accountability and support measures?
Make it stick	How can we ensure the change is sustained? How can we make the change a cultural shift? How is it going to become the core of who we are?

EEF Implementation Plan

We might also look at the Education Endowment Foundation's implementation plan when we come to this work (EEF, n.d.; Figure 6.1). This implementation plan differs from Kotter's initial eight-step model in that it focuses on initiating an exploration phase, which is followed by preparation, delivery and sustaining. One of the aspects we might consider closely is how 'amenable to change' your organisation is in terms of diversifying the curriculum, as, rightly, it is pointed out that without exploring this first, the rest of the implementation plan is at risk. We may want to consider what implementation data look like when we diversify the curriculum. One might argue that couching this work in quantitative data places a colonial lens on the work. We might seek to look at the qualitative more closely.

You may question how much time should be given to this work – after all, schools have competing priorities and often shifting landscapes. It is absolutely clear to me that the process of diversifying the curriculum is not one that can happen in a matter of months. Put simply, if unhelpfully, it takes as long as it takes. What is clear is that if we put in the time it deserves, then the outcome will be far more successful.

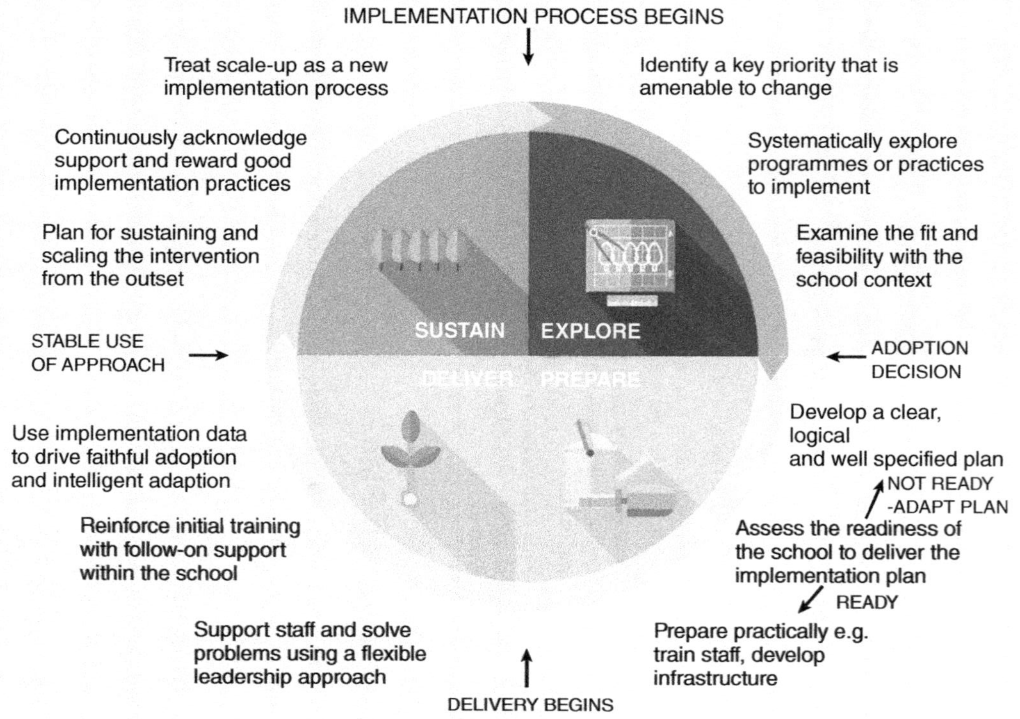

IMPLEMENTATION PROCESS BEGINS

Identify a key priority that is amenable to change

Systematically explore programmes or practices to implement

Examine the fit and feasibility with the school context

ADOPTION DECISION

Develop a clear, logical and well specified plan

NOT READY -ADAPT PLAN

Assess the readiness of the school to deliver the implementation plan

READY

Prepare practically e.g. train staff, develop infrastructure

EXPLORE

PREPARE

SUSTAIN

DELIVER

DELIVERY BEGINS

Treat scale-up as a new implementation process

Continuously acknowledge support and reward good implementation practices

Plan for sustaining and scaling the intervention from the outset

STABLE USE OF APPROACH

Use implementation data to drive faithful adoption and intelligent adaption

Reinforce initial training with follow-on support within the school

Support staff and solve problems using a flexible leadership approach

Figure 6.1 EEF implementation plan

You might want to consider the cycle of curriculum development as a first port of call. Then you might consider the pinch points in a year – what might prevent effective efforts to diversify the curriculum in terms of time?

My best advice is to sit and plan out a trajectory, knowing that it might change as you go. Where this work has been done well, it has been part of a three-to-five year cycle of curriculum development, and even then, it has been reviewed as part of an iterative cycle.

Audit and Evaluation

Any curriculum review begins with having the right information in front of you. In one of my schools, I started the curriculum review process by collating the content of the school curriculum, painstakingly copying into a spreadsheet the teaching topics for each year group, in each half term, by subject. What was an onerous task ended up being one of the most useful documents I had compiled in a school. I could now look at the curriculum in one place; I could make connections, chart sequencing for logic, see repetition and assess whether revisiting content was at greater depth. I could see cross-curricular links more easily and assess how that crossover worked. More importantly, I could have conversations with my curriculum leads about the development of knowledge over time.

So, instead of having 30 sheets of paper, each with a long- or medium-term plan on it, I had a single map of content. It was clear to me that this spreadsheet did not give me nuance, just surface level information, but it was a starting point for useful conversations.

One of the first actions I undertook was to assess the presence of marginalised groups within the curriculum. Sure enough, I found that there was basic representation of some of those groups: in the teaching of the Middle Passage, in references to colonisation and empire, in references to the fight for suffrage, in some texts, in references to statutory content on religions. Disability presence seemed limited barring a lesson or two in PSHE. Sexuality appeared briefly in PSHE, and in Religious Studies in reference to religious views on LGBT people and relationships. What was most interesting was the mode of representation. I saw that the majority of diversity in the curriculum was filtered through the lens of victimhood.

Table 6.2   Presence vs modes of representation

Presence	Mode of representation
The existence of marginalised groups in the curriculum	The lens through which marginalised groups are presented in the curriculum

The audit process, if you undertake it, has to take into account not just presence, but modes of representation (Table 6.2). These modes of representation create the sticky narratives that can formulate a young person's social schema.

If women in your curriculum are a footnote, what do our young women learn about being a woman in the world? If you are a Black teenager with African heritage, do you only ever learn about the history of oppression? What is the narrative about disability if disability is not present in the curriculum meaningfully?

Monitoring and Accountability

Everyone plays a role in the curriculum, so it stands to reason that everyone has the responsibility to make sure it is the best curriculum for your context and the young people in it. This section outlines the possibilities in interrogating the curriculum and who might ask the important questions.

Governors

School governors can have a hugely important role in ensuring that the curriculum is quality assured. While some school governors may not understand all the intricacies of the curriculum, it is important that the governing body have a working understanding of how knowledge works in society. A good example of a governing body working on reviewing the curriculum took place at one of my schools. Governors requested an audit of how the protected characteristics in the Equality Act 2010 were represented through the mainstream lessons we delivered in school. The process of auditing the curriculum in this way allowed the senior leadership team to assess the presence of anti-discriminatory work in the curriculum and allowed them to assess what representation looked like in subjects across the board.

Governors might want to ask:

- What approach do you take to diversify and decolonise the curriculum?
- How do you know children have a full working understanding of the Equality Act 2010 and protected characteristics?
- How are staff supported to develop their subject knowledge when it comes to diverse and decolonised content?

Senior Leaders

The *influence* of senior leaders is much wider than many members of staff in the rest of the school. This often means that senior leaders have impact where it comes to curriculum design, quality assurance and content decisions. In working closely with middle leaders responsible for subject areas, senior leaders are able to hold to account those who are building schemes of work and individual lessons, and the questions senior leaders can ask will often drive curriculum change in a strategic manner.

Mary Myatt and John Tomsett (2021) explore the idea of subject line management in their excellent book entitled *Huh*. In this they encourage senior leaders who are not subject specialists to become more familiar with the nuances of individual subjects and they encourage them to pull on threads of enquiry during line management meetings. Just as you would question the way assessment or resource design is used in a subject, a senior leader can be responsible for questioning the way that particular content is taught. For example, if you manage the history subject leader, you may want to know the following:

- What approach do we take when teaching empire?
- How do we teach about the history of disability?
- When we teach the American West, how do we refer to the indigenous peoples of America?
- When we teach about the Middle Passage, how far do we acknowledge the role of the United Kingdom in a way that examines culpability?

An effective line management meeting is not just about data, it requires dialogue about the way in which we choose to teach topics, who we choose to include and how we challenge thinking about the world that we live in.

Subject Leaders

Subject leaders are the spine of a school setting. In many ways, the subject leader's knowledge and expertise in diversity, equity and inclusion can make or break efforts to diversify the curriculum. It is often the work of a well-informed subject leader that will spur team members on to look at their own subject knowledge when it comes to topics where diversity in the curriculum may be appropriate. Subject leaders have a responsibility to keep informed about the language of diversity, the implications of social change on the topics being taught in the curriculum and the context of their school population and how that might influence the way topics are taught.

If you are a subject leader, you may want to consider the following:

- How do the topics taught in your subject reflect the world we live in today?
- How far are your team members aware of how to teach 'tricky' content?
- What opportunities are there to design curriculum sequences that are logical and diverse?
- Who are the significant figures we cover and what do we need to know about them?

Classroom Teachers

In a world where lesson plans are often centralised, it might seem a daunting task to think about diversity in the lessons you have been asked to teach. Often the best way to work with centralised resources is to think of them as a skeleton for the lesson you are about to deliver. You have scope to adjust the learning to meet the needs of your classroom and that might mean considering the following:

- How well informed am I about the implications of what I am teaching when it comes to diversity, equity and inclusion?
- How much have I considered the images, the examples, the stories, the references and the language of this lesson in order to provide a wide-ranging view of the world?
- How prepared am I for questions, or to address misconceptions about people, places, ideas and cultures in relation to what I am teaching?
- Am I taking an actively equitable approach when explaining aspects of protected characteristics as they come up in this sequence of learning?

If you are in the position where you are designing your lesson from scratch, then you have ample opportunity to consider the same questions as for someone with centralised resources. The conscious crafting of a lesson is a beautiful skill, and one that involves careful consideration of how you will deliver the content and make sure it is retained without misconception. It may be the case that you have opportunity to craft questions that challenge common myths.

Teaching Assistants

The teaching assistant really does have the bird's eye view of what is happening in class-rooms across the school. Who else has the opportunity to be present in the classroom across a range of subjects with a range of students with wildly different characteristics on a daily basis? Teaching assistants can be hugely useful in evaluating the messages that are delivered by the curriculum across subjects; it is a hugely powerful position to hold. Although teaching assistants may not feel like they have a large sphere of influence, if they work in a school where staff voice is considered useful, then support staff can feed-back their ideas on how certain things are taught. If an opportunity arises for a support member of staff to provide feedback on the curriculum the following might be raised:

- I've noticed in PSHE that all references to relationships are heterosexual.
- I've noticed that students have developed some archaic ideas about how to refer to indigenous peoples because of the way history units are taught.
- I've noticed that girls in PE are not able to play the sports that they are interested in because they are deemed to be 'boys' sports'.
- I've noticed that all the artists we study in Art are Western European.

Students, Parents and the Community

Students are *sometimes* very perceptive about the content of their curriculum and how it is taught. We often hesitate to ask them how the curriculum is being received because there remains a belief in some circles that students cannot possibly have the skills, or even the language, to evaluate the curriculum effectively. The choices that are made for them are made by professionals and these choices could not possibly be questioned effectively or to a purposeful endpoint by those who sit in our classrooms. Research by Brown et al. (2019) suggests that there are three reasons why we as educators might refrain from conducting student voice.

1   Student response may be idealistic: in terms of the curriculum, students may not have a good sense of academic content and may choose to avoid what they dislike, or find difficult.
2   Student response may be divided: there might be conflicting ideas about what is taught.
3   Student response might be threatening: students may request material that goes against values, statutory requirements and/or government guidance.

This does not mean that we should not ask students how the curriculum is landing with them. The process of engaging young people in their own learning requires us to start a conversation about the curriculum choices that have been made, or might be made. And as Christine Counsell points out, part of disciplinary enquiry is learning that what we teach is not all there is.

Do parents have a role? Does the community? Perhaps not in deciding what is taught. But we are responsible for consultation on RSE policies, even if we might find that there is objection to content on LGBTQ+ identities and relationships. There is always scope for conflict of belief when it comes to curriculum content; how well we field the conversation is a determiner of our commitment to collaboration and inclusion.

Subject Knowledge Development

Increasingly, we are becoming aware that subject knowledge is vital in ensuring that our young people have access to the best curriculum they can experience. Coe et al. (2014) highlighted the impact of subject knowledge on outcomes. When considering diverse content, subject knowledge development is key.

How does your organisation prioritise subject knowledge development? In many education settings, we are expected to hold department meetings, and as many of you will recognise, that time is often taken up by the administrative aspects of our roles. In one of the schools I worked in, I wanted to shift the focus away from those admin tasks and to move towards a sense of enquiry about subject knowledge. I noticed there was some directed time available that could be adapted for subject knowledge purposes.

So, after I appropriated that hour, I spoke to middle leaders about what needed to happen in that protected time. Discussions should be purely based on subject knowledge related to what is being taught. I emphasised the need for staff to go away and research diversity in the curriculum, alongside all the other facets of teaching a particular topic, and to come back and share that knowledge in the hour given.

I fondly recall the first English session. We were teaching a lot of Shakespeare that half term. I went away and researched aspects of *A Midsummer Night's Dream*, in particular the significance of the little blue boy at the centre of Titania and Oberon's squabbles. I came back with information on how that little blue boy was not a random manifestation, but a reference to colonial interests (highly significant that he has blue skin, because of the depiction of Indian demi-gods as having blue skin). Titania and Oberon were not just two peevish foes, but colonial powers fighting over their economic interests in South Asia. Another member of staff came back with the significance of equivocation in *Macbeth*. Someone else looked at representations of women. It was fruitful. Most of all, it was huge amounts of fun.

To do subject knowledge development well, teachers need access to resources. Having a bank of signposted resources can kickstart the process of adapting the curriculum.

I am immensely lucky to have read the work of, and engaged with, some brilliant organisations that support us in developing our subject knowledge. Of course, the resource bank below is not exhaustive, but merely a starting point for you to use on developing your own subject knowledge so that you can adapt your curriculum effectively.

Websites

- The Black Curriculum – https://theblackcurriculum.com
- British Ugandan Asians at 50 – www.bua50.org
- Brown History (paid) – https://brownhistory.substack.com
- Decolonising Geography – https://decolonisegeography.com
- Digital Transgender Archive – www.digitaltransgenderarchive.net
- The Jewish Women's Archive – https://jwa.org
- Lit in Colour – www.penguin.co.uk/lit-in-colour
- Our Migration Story – www.ourmigrationstory.org.uk
- RomArchive (Roma History) – www.romarchive.eu/en/
- Schools Out (LGBT Resources) – https://lgbtplushistorymonth.co.uk
- UK Disability History Month – https://ukdhm.org
- Windrush Foundation – https://windrushfoundation.com

Books

- *African Europeans: An Untold History* – Olivette Otele
- *Black and British* – David Olusoga
- *Braiding Sweetgrass: Indigenous Wisdom, Scientific Knowledge and The Teachings of Plants* – Robin Wall Kimmerer
- *The Crest of the Peacock: Non-European Roots of Mathematics* – George Joseph
- *Decolonising the English Literary Curriculum* – eds. Ato Quayson and Ankhi Mukherjee
- *Disability Visibility: First-Person Stories from the Twenty-first Century* – ed. Alice Wong

- *Femina* – Janina Ramirez
- *The Stopping Places* – Damien Le Bas
- *The Whole Picture: The Colonial Story of the Art in our Museums and Why We Need to Talk About it* – Alice Proctor

Associations and Subject Support (Active in Diversity Strategies)

The Historical Association – www.history.org.uk

The Geographical Association – https://geography.org.uk

The English Association – https://englishassociation.ac.uk

The National Association for Teaching English (NATE) – www.nate.org.uk

The Association for Science Education – www.ase.org.uk

National Society for Education in Art and Design (NSEAD) – www.nsead.org

....**REFLECTION QUESTIONS**

- How familiar are you with change models and how to apply them to curriculum adaptation?
- What tangible steps need to take place before you start this journey?
- How will you ensure that people are on board with you?
- What sources of support are you familiar with to signpost for others?

....

7

EXPANDING THE BOUNDARIES

We are products of our own education. The National Curriculum, instituted in my early schooling, held very few references to global knowledge. This is not particularly surprising. The Swann Report in 1985 provided guidance on the need to account for the growing multicultural school population, in that it expressed 'the government is firmly committed to the principle that all children, irrespective of race, colour or ethnic origin, should have a good education which develops their abilities and aptitudes to the full and brings about a true sense of belonging to Britain' (www.education-uk.org, n.d.). This did not provide a mandate for global knowledge, or a decolonised knowledge base for all children. Other reports, such as the one by Olneck in 2001, actively expressed the dangers of including diverse material, in that doing so might lead to greater racial division nationally (Olneck, 2001). Most of the reports on diversity in the curriculum emphasised the need to have a curriculum that enhanced a sense of Britishness (Maylor et al., 2007).

So let us consider the boundaries, geographical and otherwise, of the knowledge we have been conditioned to value above all other knowledge. We are taught to value:

- White Western European knowledge, in particular that which is centred on Britain.
- Post-enlightenment knowledge.
- Knowledge that is northern hemisphere in origin.
- Knowledge that is generated by men.
- Knowledge that is focused on the heteronormative.
- Knowledge that centres the able-bodied.

Knowledge itself is the centre of this chapter: where it comes from, how it relates to power and colonisation and how it is used for discourses on sexuality, disability and gender, as well as for race/culture.

'The Four Epistemicides of the Long 16th Century'

Boaventura de Sousa Santos outlines four 'killings of knowledge' or epistemicides of what he calls the long 16th century. The result is an erasure of global and indigenous knowledge that may have formed a significantly greater impact on our society. In their article, Hall and Tandon (2017: 11) define the four epistemicides:

(1) the conquest of Al-Andalus, and the expulsion of Muslims and Jews from Europe,

(2) the conquest of the Indigenous Peoples of the Americas started by the Spanish, continued by the French and the English and still underway today,

(3) the creation of the slave trade that resulted in millions being killed in Africa and at sea, and more being totally dehumanized by enslavement in the Americas

(4) the killing of millions of Indo-European women, mostly through burning at the stake as witches because their knowledge practices were not controlled by men.

What would be the impact on our knowledge, or epistemologies, if Al-Andalus had not been 're-conquered' by the Spanish in the late 1500s? What would we study and learn about and value? What knowledge would we still have access to if the Indigenous peoples of the Americas had remained free and unconquered? What understanding would we have of our world if African knowledge had not been subject to erasure through enslavement? What place would womanhood and femininity have in the curriculum, if women's 'deviant' knowledge had not been deemed so and erased?

Ideas about where knowledge should come from and how it should be transmitted through the curriculum are rooted in a deep-seated racism. Michael Baker, citing Enrique Dussel, writes that 'Modern (European) civilization understands itself as the most developed, the superior, civilization. This sense of superiority obliges it, in the form of a categorical imperative, as it were, to "develop" (civilize, uplift, educate) the more primitive, barbarous, underdeveloped civilizations' (Baker, 2012: 4). He goes on to state: 'The cognate concepts civility, civilizing, and civilization are part of the modern categorial matrix through which modern schooling and European identity were constituted' (Baker, 2012: 6)

The Boundaries of Gender

It is hard to know how to construct a field of knowledge that is centred on women in the same way that it has been centred on men. On conducting research on what knowledge generated by and owned by women might even be, I found myself meeting barrier after barrier. Because of patriarchy, and the way in which women have been excluded from epistemologies, we find ourselves having to consider what women's knowledge even means to us now.

One way to look at women's knowledge and power comes in the form of learning about matriarchal societies. This could be looked at in PSHE, or in Sociology lessons. It could form a case study in Geography. We could look at one of the largest matrilineal societies globally, the Minangkabau in West Sumatra, where 4 million people live in a matrilineal society. Islam is practised as the dominant religion. Inheritance is passed down between women, and while men can hold leadership positions, it is women who are the centre of the community.

Women's roles in medicine and healing can offer a pathway to consider how, despite being excluded from 'medicine' as a scientific endeavour, women's knowledge has been developed and passed on. Minkowski (1992) outlines the extensive role women played in public health in England, until Henry V's 1421 decree that women were no longer to be engaged in medical work. Women healers have existed across cultures – and were observed as such by Western European visitors. The World Health Organization (2023) cites the example of Lady Mary Wortley Motto witnessing, in 1721, the practice of inoculation in Greek and Armenian women and using this to inoculate her own child against smallpox.

Indigenous Views on Sexuality

One of the ways that we can bring indigenous knowledge into the curriculum is to reference indigenous views on sexuality. When teaching about gender and sexuality, it is worth referencing how cultures have grappled with concepts of binary/non-binary. An example of this might be in the existence of language that incorporates non-binary identities. Picq and Tikuna (2019) highlight the fact that 'In Juchitán, Mexico, *muxes* are neither man nor woman, but a Zapotec gender hybridity.' The writers emphasise that the colonial impact on language about gender and sexuality is enormous, citing the example of Ancient Zapotec not having concepts of he/she until the arrival of the Spanish conquistadores.

Another example of expanding the boundaries of knowledge on sexuality is by referencing figures like We'wha, known for being a Lhamana (Zuni Two-Spirit person). Mariana Brandman explains:

> Though born a male-bodied person, community members recognized that We'wha demonstrated traits associated with the lhamana as early as age three or four. In Zuni culture, lhamana (now more often described with the pan-Indian term 'Two Spirit') were male-bodied individuals who took on social and ceremonial roles generally performed by women. They usually, though not exclusively, wore women's clothing and mostly took up labors associated with women. Lhamana constituted a socially-recognized third gender role within the tribe and often held positions of honor in the community. (Brandman, 2021)

A final example comes from South Asia. The famous carvings at the temple of Khajuraho is noted for its depictions of sexuality, including sculptures of same-sex sexual activity. There is a field of work on the queer history of South Asia that will also tell you about the acknowledgement of gender fluidity. Vishavjeet Dhaliwal (2023) explains: 'We can see this worldview reflected in the Vedas (c. 1500 BCE–500 BCE), the foundational texts of Hinduism and South Asian culture. The texts categorizes people as one of three genders – male (*purusha-prakriti*), female (*stri-prakriti*) or third gender (*tritiya-prakriti*), the latter group consisting of people who did not fit into male or female.'

Indeed, the existence of a third gender is evident in modern life. Hijra are often assigned male at birth, or can be intersex. They are recognised under Indian law as a third gender and afforded some protections.

Here we have put our pins in Central America, in North America and in India, all under the umbrella of gender and sexuality. That is a brilliant expansion of boundaries.

Expanding Religious Studies and Philosophy

The gathering and transmission of knowledge were not always centred on Western Europe. As we know, many of our core concepts of Maths and Science came from ideas and observations made in India, China and the Middle East. Take Schopenhauer (not a figure that usually makes it into the curriculum, but one for illustrative purposes only). His philosophy was indelibly influenced by the *Upanishads* and the *Vedas*, by his own admission. Schopenhauer found inspiration outside of the Western European hegemony to strengthen his own thoughts, to develop and to grow his philosophy. In Urs App's study of the connection, he cites Schopenhauer:

> At the same time, the orientalist Friedrich Majer introduced me, without solicitation, to Indian antiquity, and this had an essential influence on me.
>
> [*Zugleich führte, unaufgefordert, der Orientalist Friedrich Majer mich in das Indische Alterthum ein, welches von we- sentlichem Einfluß auf mich gewesen ist.*] (Letter to Johann Eduard Erdmann of 9 April, 1851, in Hübscher (ed.), 1987; in App, 2006)

In Religious Studies, we have the opportunity to draw links between our most common religious stories. When we reference the making of 'man' (or mankind), we are familiar with the story of Adam and Eve. Where else can we find narratives of the first man and the first woman? Possibly in the Manu myths of India, or perhaps also in the Maori myths of Tāne – a woman said to be the first human. There is also an opportunity to look at the way flood narratives cross cultures: from the flood of Noah, to the flood myth of Akkadian culture – that of Enlil destroying the world with a flood because humans had become too troublesome.

Using Literature to Expand Boundaries

It is not remarkable then that I taught according to the prevailing values of the time in my early days as a teacher. As an English teacher, I used to teach Greek and Roman myths in an attempt to increase my students' understanding of intertextuality – the concept of literature being a conversation in which writers referred to each other's works.

This was not a terrible idea. My students benefited from seeing how certain tropes appeared in texts across time; they saw how symbols were referencing ideas that had come before. If you understand that Arachne was challenged to a weaving contest by Minerva and on her death was transformed into a spider, you not only understand the aetiology of spiders' webs, you recognise that a character knitting or weaving to save their own life is a call back to an earlier story.

The problem was that my reach was almost entirely Eurocentric, in part due to my own lack of knowledge about how texts build on each other; certainly, my knowledge on how texts 'speak' to each other was stunted by my own lack of education on the history of global literature. At school I didn't learn about anything beyond Greek mythology (and even that was superficial).

It was only when I was researching epic poetry as part of my teaching that I came across the *Epic of Gilgamesh* (2100 BC–1800 BC). If you have never read it, it is a Sumerian epic poem whose eponymous hero precedes Odysseus as the protagonist of *The Odyssey* (said to have originated in the 7th or 8th century BC) of Greek epic literature. Both heroes, Gilgamesh and Odysseus, are leaders who take journeys, visit the underworld, fight gods and monsters and visit enchanted spaces. They are both said to possess an arrogance that leads to deception at various points of both texts. In 'The Gilgamesh Epic and Homer', Gresseth (1975: 2) defines the convergence of the two heroes as a 'line ... traceable from the Sumerian materials from which the Akkadian epic was formed to the world of Homer'.

What struck me was this idea of the 'traceable line'. How does literature cross time and space to replicate itself? What is the human connection that drives this replication? Of course, the two spaces are relatively geographically connected – Ancient Mesopotamia and Ancient Greece are not separated in the way that the UK is from Australia. Moving people often transport with them their stories. Ultimately, what I saw here was the way in which humans, regardless of the culture, shared the same concerns about the human condition – what it meant to be human in a world of divine beings.

By teaching both to my students, I placed a pin on the world map into Iraq, as well as Greece. When I taught them about Beowulf, I pinned Northern Europe. If you had to put a pin in the map for where the knowledge in your subject originates from, how far and how wide would your pins be spread?

Using History and Geography to Expand Boundaries

This expanding of geographical boundaries does not have to be limited to literature. When we teach about feudalism, we often teach it as a uniquely British concept, through omission rather than as a deliberate obfuscation. But feudal structures exist globally; one only has to take a quick look into Japanese feudal structures under the Shoguns to see that while the categories of stratified society are labelled differently, the structure is remarkably similar. Some scholars also cite the Zagwe dynasty of Ethiopia as functioning with a feudal system. So why is it that we limit children's understanding of the concept to one geographical space? The connections are remarkable and speak to global organisations of society.

On the simplest level, what we are seeing here is the opportunity to connect people and places. The British child, the child of Japanese heritage and the Ethiopian child have something in common that is a part of our history and development as a human race. Belonging can be created through this connection.

In Geography, we have the opportunity to look at how humans have shaped their environment. In looking at water management, we can look at *qanat* water-management systems in the Middle East and in Africa. We can examine their impact on the environment. We can look at Byzantine Constantinople's agricultural successes that led to food security even in times of war.

An interesting angle posed by Puttick and Murrey (2022) is that of using 'parodies' to highlight the colonial lens of geography. They cite the example of Milton Allimadi's 'discovery' of a river, which he names 'River Gulu'. The parody here is that he is in London and is looking at the Thames. What might a student learn from this parody of exploration and discovery?

1   How does History teaching show the connectedness of society?
2   Where do students learn the colonial and patriarchal slants of History and Geography?
3   Where are the missing pins? What aspects of global history and geography are missing (and needed)?

Expanding Art and Music

As mentioned previously, becoming culturally literate was at the heart of E.D. Hirsch's thinking. In *Cultural Literacy: What Every American Should Know* (1987: xiii), he states: 'To be culturally literate is to possess the basic information needed to thrive in the modern world.' What then is the reach of this basic information?

In order to understand how Eurocentric narratives have affected our understanding of what constitutes art, let us turn our attention back to how art was taught to us in school. My understanding and appreciation of art was through famous paintings and painters – and I list those embedded in my memory: Degas, Monet, Turner, Constable.

Where does art come from? Who invented it? Who was 'best' at it? To whom do we attribute artistic merit today?

It is clear that in primary art education, there is a real move to decolonise art and show that it is a global phenomenon. In the best examples of diversity in the Art curriculum, we see appearances by artists of all cultures and abilities, genders and sexualities. Women feature more often than they have done in the past. There is a sense that art is universal, which begs the question: why is art universal, but not literature, or maths?

Even though art as a subject is less prescribed than English Literature, we might want to consider the ways in which art is a product of colonial thinking. It is clear that art from global communities is studied, for example Aboriginal art features on many a curriculum. Its positionality is interesting. It is situated at the start of the curriculum, as an introduction to line, shape, colour, or does it sit within units of work that occur later, when students have acquired their basic skills? In this, we see a fundamental misunderstanding of the value of Aboriginal art – its symbolism, its significance and its story. We can paint a similar picture in work done on African masks, or Day of the Dead art.

In Music, we often see 'world music' as part of the curriculum. Of course, this works on a basic level to 'expand the boundaries' of music as a discipline; but there are problematic aspects we may need to reflect on. How far is the inclusion of world music an activity in 'tourism', rather than a distinct exercise in meaning through music? Hess (2015: 341) suggests that rather than have a Music model in which world culture is inserted as an 'also', we might look at the comparative musics model:

> Repositioning this model as the Comparative Musics Model, a music curriculum following this model would not take an additive approach to music education. Nor would it assume that only 'Other' musics are worthy of study, normalizing Western classical music in the process. Rather, such a course would be taught as a comparative course that emphasizes the interconnectedness between the musics and the contexts of the musics. It is also attentive to power relations.

This approach ensures that when we do put a pin in the world map of culture, we are doing so with careful consideration of how global art and music have been positioned over the centuries. This ensures that we are also looking at the way power works in those subjects.

1   Where and when are global references in Art or Music placed in your curriculum?
2   How much does the study of global Art or Music focus on the inherent value of the product, rather than the 'otherness' of the product?
3   How is language employed when considering global Art and Music? Is it described with value and with conceptual clarity?

Expanding Maths

It is difficult to assess how and when we would teach the history of Mathematics, but a sense of place and time is important in considering the 'narrative' of the subject itself. When we teach about place value, when do we introduce the contribution of ancient Indian mathematics? How do we explain the impact of the Ancient Mesopotamian sexagesimal system on how we tell the time, or measure angles in a circle? Mathematics is a global endeavour, with global roots and branches, but most people will go through their lives attributing its development to post-Enlightenment Europe. Another example that might appear in your lessons is the Ishango bone of central Africa, that is said to date back 20,000 years. While anthropologists, mathematicians and archaeologists disagree as to the exact use of the bone, which features what some have considered to be tally marks, it is broadly understood that the bone represents an early engagement with mathematics. The impact of highlighting how far Mathematics has travelled over time and geography is clear. Maths is for everyone and from everyone. It belongs in you too.

1   What parallels can be found in the knowledge said to originate in Western Europe and that which may have originated elsewhere?
2   How do we show that our subjects cross geographical boundaries?
3   How can we make relevant concepts and knowledge that come from cultures outside of our own?

Expanding Engineering and Design

The achievement of Britain is centred in the curriculum, which can be understood if we take the view that we are educating our young people to believe in the exceptionality of Britain. If we look at how British endeavour appears in the curriculum, we might see Stonehenge being afforded a mythological status, what English Heritage calls a 'unique prehistoric monument' on their website. The reality is that there are hundreds, if not thousands, of these megaliths across Europe, possibly appearing due to the endeavours of a single hunter-gatherer population originating in Brittany over 7000 years ago. Stonehenge dates as far back as 2000 BC, and we learn about it in primary school, foregoing megalithic sites such as Gobekli Tepe, a megalithic site dating back to 9500 BC with far more complexity than that of Stonehenge. There are two things to be considered here: are we inadvertently creating the misconception that Stonehenge is a masterpiece that could only be created here? And are we downplaying the importance of global megaliths, and the ingenuity of their construction, because they are not British?

We might feel more comfortable, because we are products of our education, referencing the pyramids in Egypt as a feat of engineering and design. When we look at structures, how they are constructed and made strong, we might also reference pyramidical structures in other cultures, notably the Ziggurat at Ur. What is it that draws people to certain designs? It is largely believed that humans have constructed these edifices in the image of nature, in particular, mountains.

Key questions to ask:

1   Where can you find examples of engineering feats from different cultures?
2   How can we explore innovation and design from a cross-section of society?
3   How can we take a comparative approach to looking at design, architecture and engineering?

Expanding Sport and PE

If football is the great national sport (and I am more than happy to have this debated), we could look at how games that are seen as British may have roots elsewhere. We may also look at the universality of invasion games in general. The history of football often starts in the medieval period, and yet we can find examples of similar games as early as 3000 years ago in Mesoamerica, where a proto-football was played with a rubber ball. We can also reference the game of *cuju* played in China.

What would be the point? The games we teach in PE have cultural significance and, yes, we need to learn how to play them and be physically adept at them, but there is value in knowing that our games have evolved over time and place to become the games as we know them now. Certainly with the association between football and nationalism, we can show that football (in its various guises) is a game that transcends cultures.

1   How do the games we know and love exist elsewhere in the world?
2   What echoes can we find in the sports that we study in other countries?
3   Why do some nations take on particular sports as national interests and others do not?

.... **REFLECTION QUESTIONS**

1   To what extent is your curriculum globally focused?
2   How can you ensure that global content is not 'exoticised'?
3   What aspects of your curriculum are bound by colonial, patriarchal and heteronormative structures?

....

8

PARALLEL STORIES AND PAIRED TEXTS

When I meet teachers and deliver training on diversifying the curriculum, I am conscious that there might be a perception that in diversifying, we are stating that there is no room for white western narratives. This is simply not the case. I have argued over the years that the most effective way to diversify the curriculum is to look at the ways in which Western European knowledge speaks to global knowledge and that there is a need for conscious crafting of the curriculum that results in a coherent and, indeed, beautiful iteration of curriculum for young people.

One way that we can consider this crafting is through the medium of paralleling stories, and pairing texts. By allowing the idea that narratives have equal merit and do not have to be placed in a hierarchy, we can start to redistribute power as it has previously been manifested. We have been perhaps guilty of only providing a single story in terms of achievement, understanding, experience and contribution.

Single Stories

Sometimes, you come across a TED Talk that alters the way you think about the world. My first experience of this was when I watched a three-minute snippet on how we have been tying our shoelaces wrongly our whole lives. Then I watched Chimamanda Ngozi Adichie's TED Talk entitled *The Danger of a Single Story*. While I am known to be occasionally effusive, this moment called for effusiveness. I heard it. I heard her talk about what happens when people are not educated roundly. In the talk, so eloquently delivered, Adichie talks about how stories can come to define people and places – especially those outside of a white, western lens. She states:

> This single story of Africa ultimately comes, I think, from Western literature. Now, here is a quote from the writing of a London merchant called John Locke, who sailed to west Africa in 1561, and kept a fascinating account of his voyage. After referring to the black Africans as 'beasts who have no houses,' he writes, 'They are also people without heads, having their mouth and eyes in their breasts.'

In telling this distorted story, Locke becomes a cog in the machine that churns out versions of this tale. The African as exotic, dangerous, primitive and so on. He is not the only one who has chosen to present the fictive version of a story representing Africans this way.

In designing a curriculum, we choose a pathway through the content and it is most decidedly a choice, influenced by the prevailing ideas about knowledge in our society. Our society prefers a narrative about non-white cultures that reinforces a racist culture, because it keeps those without power and influence without power and influence.

Take the example of Australian history. What is the story that we learn? If studied at all, we are told that convicts were shipped to Australia (the quintessential *terra nullius*) and that they founded a colony there. It is not hard to find the narratives of Aboriginal peoples who were there through this process of colonialism. We can provide their narratives and viewpoints (where available). We can start to look at the process of colonisation through their eyes. Through the paralleling of stories, we can learn about colonial settlers and figures such as Bennelong, or Pemulwuy, or Bungaree.

A story told within the curriculum can be seen as the 'only' narrative, or part of a wider, more complex web of stories. Our role as designers means that we have it within our control to deliver more than one perspective on people, places, events and cultures.

Multiperspectivity in History

Multiperspectivity is an important aspect of teaching History, in particular. In the work of Wansink et al. (2018: 496) we are informed that 'over the past 25 years, the term multiperspectivity has gained importance in history education. In the context of history education, the notion of multiperspectivity refers to the epistemological idea that history is interpretational and subjective, with multiple coexisting narratives about particular historical events, rather than history being objectively represented by one "closed" narrative.'

What closed narratives do we expose young people to?

We can look at the way in which the story of World War I is told in schools at various points of a child's education. I learned about the horrors of WWI through History, English Literature, PSHE and through the marking of Armistice Day without fail every year. I was appalled by the death, moved to commemorate, but it was someone else's story. My family, my people, anyone with brown skin had not been involved, so I could appropriately and respectfully mark the tragedy of the loss of life, but it was one story.

In my twenties, I visited, as an adult, the battlefields of Flanders with a tour guide who could only be described as eccentric. We did the big cemeteries, with their luminous Portland stone monuments. Then he took us to Langemarck. If you've never been, it's a sad, bleak little plot full to the brim of the bodies of dead German soldiers. Boys, most of them, not even men, in mass graves, with no pomp. Portland stone was reserved for the victors. These men made do with a heavy grey stone, marked only by one sculpture of soldiers with their heads downturned, shoulders dropped, to signify their shame.

The point of this is that the story suddenly had a new perspective. The tragedy was not just a British one, but a German one too. They were people too, lying here in the cold February ground on a day that could be best described as Baltic. I began looking for the hidden stories that ran parallel to the one I had been told. The First World War was a British triumph, not a global one. But then crept in the faces of brown soldiers, turbaned and armed, sitting in hotter climes, fighting the same battle. Then came the stories of brown skinned and black skinned people wielding weapons for 'the mother-land'. Then came their letters and poetry, their accounts of skirmishes, shells, mud – such as this letter from Isher Singh:

> The battle is being carried on very bitterly. In the Lahore Division only 300 men are left. Some are dead, some wounded. The division is finished. Think of it – in taking 50 yards of German trench, 50,000 men are killed. When we attack they direct a terrific fire on us – thousands of men die daily. It looks as if not a single man can remain alive on either side – then (when none is left) there will be peace... (Isher Singh [Sikh, 59th Rifles] to a friend [50th Punjabi, Punjab] wrote in Gurmukhi on 1 May 1915 from Indian General Hospital, Brighton describing the war of New Chappelle, SikhNet, 2009)

The experiences of Black soldiers from the West Indies are also widely available. The Voices of War and Peace website has a large collection of sources that can be used as a parallel to the experiences of white soldiers, as exemplified here by Norman Manley:

> I had grown up with horses and horse-drawn vehicles, and knew more about them than miners and town-bred Londoners, so naturally enough within a month I was a Lance Corporal or Bombardier as they were called in the Artillery, and by the time we left for France I was promoted Corporal. Here I came up against violent colour prejudice. The rank and file disliked taking orders from a coloured N.C.O. and their attitude was mild by comparison with that of my fellow NCOs. Corporals and Sergeants resented my sharing status with them. (Manley, 1973: 1–2)

The parallel stories of women can be sought out too. When I first taught poetry from the First World War, the only woman's voice was often that of Jessie Pope, the infamous female Pied Piper, drawing young men to their deaths through her siren-call poetry. Her poetry now reads like a warning about women's callousness.

> Who's for the game, the biggest that's played,
>
> The red crashing game of a fight?
>
> Who'll grip and tackle the job unafraid?
>
> And who thinks he'd rather sit tight?
>
> 'Who's For the Game?' Jessie Pope (1915)

Hearing about women in battle, on the frontlines, as nurses, dressed up as men at times – that was new to me. I had not heard of Edith Cavell, or Dorothy Lawrence. I had only read poetry pining for lost men. The concept that woman had agency and power in the First World War developed in adulthood; but by then the idea that British men had saved the world entirely by themselves had formed and congealed. It is hard to shift a narrative that is embedded and reinforced in childhood.

In *Forgotten Voices* (Arthur, 2012: 67), we hear first-hand accounts of women's experiences in WWI, such as this excerpt from Mrs M. Hall:

> I'd never been in a factory before, but the crisis made you think. I thought well, my brother and my friends are in France, so a friend and I thought to ourselves, well, let's do something. So we wrote to London and asked for war work. And we directed to a munitions factory at Perivale in London. We had to have a health examination because we had to be physically fit – perfect eyesight and strong. We had to supply four references and be British-born of British parents.

This extract counters the 'Eve' figure narrative of Jessie Pope and women waving white feathers. A parallel story that serves more than one purpose.

Multiperspectivity in Geography

Another way to consider this is by examining the idea of multiperspectivity in Geography. In my book *A Little Guide for Teachers: Diversity in Schools* (Kara, 2020) I touch upon this idea and I intend to expand upon it here. It is a simple idea: when we introduce a concept that involves national or geographical significance, we have the opportunity to include the perspectives of a range of different people.

An example might by in presenting the impact of a natural disaster. We could ask the following questions:

- Whose voices are heard on this event?
- Whose voices have traditionally been unheard in relation to this event?
- How can we draw on sources to provide 'multiple coexisting narratives'? (Wansink et al., 2018)

The work of the Center for Disaster Philanthropy (CDP) takes an equitable approach when reporting on the impact of all forms of disaster. It examines already existing inequalities and shows how those inequalities are exacerbated in the event of a natural disaster. On their website, there is a detailed breakdown of how women face a multitude of serious effects compared to their male counterparts. The CDP references the research of the World Bank in examining the impact of disaster on women (Carlsson Rex and Trohanis, 2012); notably:

- In some cases, where inequality exists in society, women are more likely to die in the event of a natural disaster.

- Sexual violence goes unreported, or is reported very slowly.
- Women who are pregnant or undergoing childbirth are at serious risk of harm (CDP, n.d.).

The field of Geography allows for multiple perspectives across a range of headings. In resources produced by National Geographic, we are asked to explore geographical ideas as shown in Table 8.1. I have added in questions to support interpretation for the curriculum.

Table 8.1 Multiperspective approaches to Geography

	Questions	Curriculum
Spatial	Why is it there? What is it near?	Significance of rivers on different groups
Cultural	How do people relate to it? How are relationships influenced?	Religious buildings and local geography
Political	What policies are in place? Who controls them?	Childbirth policies and populations in relation to people with disabilities
Economic	How are resources distributed? What are the costs and benefits?	Industry and impact on women in particular regions
Historical	How have things stayed the same or changed over time? Who has influence over this?	Effect of growth and expansion on indigenous people
Geological	How do natural features relate to impact on different people?	Tourism and effect on Aboriginal populations in Australia
Ecological	How are species connected and how have humans impacted this?	Crop cultivation and impact on village populations

Adapted from a resource designed by National Geographic (education.nationalgeographic.org, n.d.)

It may seem difficult to plan for multiperspectivity in Science; however, there are some ways forward. In teaching about scientific discovery, we might consider the following:

- The invention of the atomic bomb was seen as a huge leap in scientific warfare. What was the impact long and short term on the Allied nations and on Japanese populations?
- If scientific observation was conducted mostly by men, how might their observations be biased towards the masculine?

Multiple Perspectives Across Subjects

We have looked in detail at History and Geography when considering multiple perspectives. How else might we use this strategy of paralleling stories?

Exploring perspectives in Science is important because culture, gender and power play a huge role in what is deemed valid. Take this example, as outlined by Medin et al.

(2014: 45): 'Lawrence Kohlberg's highly influential work on stages of moral development in children in the early 1970s was later called into question by psychologist Carol
Gilligan on the grounds that it ignored the perspective of women, who tended to
emphasize the ethic of caring. Nor did Kohlberg's model account for moral principles
associated with Eastern religious traditions, in part because his scheme did not include
principles of cooperation and nonviolence.'

The point here is that our conclusions are subject to our identity markers, despite the
assertion that science is logical, rational and supported by evidence. In the same article,
we also learn that female primates were deemed passive and monogamous until female
primatologists started observing them, and only then did the idea of active participa-
tion in mating behaviour and multiple partners take hold. Multiple perspectives add
depth and possibility to our observations of the world.

Other ideas:

- Drama – exploring events from multiple points of view, writing and performing
  monologues from underwritten characters, considering cultural approaches to
  theatre design.
- IT/Computing – the impact of computation on different societies, women's
  perspectives on development of computational software, the impact of assistive
  technology for people with disabilities.
- Religious Education – comparison of flood narratives, the impact of Christianity
  on women and people with disabilities, religious attitudes to sexuality.
- Languages – the parallel experiences of those in the Francophone world, the
  impact of language and colonisation.
- Classics – parallel narratives in antiquity, connection with pre-classical
  civilisations.
- Food – the story of tea over land and sea, the significance of food items in
  different countries.
- Textiles – chintz in India and in Britain, weaving in Europe and in Mesoamerica.
- Politics – comparing medieval politics in Europe and China, the role of women in
  politics in Britain and in matriarchal societies.

I could go on. The point I am making is that comparative study fosters critical perspectives on global culture and identity. It demonstrates the contribution of all cultures and
bodies and genders to our understanding of the world.

Creating Agency

As pointed out in Chapter 5, the inevitable tension when trying to diversify stories that
are told in school lies in the fact that so many stories of marginalised people are
couched in the narrative of victimhood. When we learn about race, gender, disability
and so on, we learn about the history of oppression – and of course, we should because

that is a reality that one cannot escape from. Women have been oppressed through the patriarchy; the global majority has experienced the terrible effect of colonisation.

Does this mean that all the narratives we construct about these groups should be limited to their victim status? Even as I write this, I hesitate to use the word 'victim', with its heavy connotations of helplessness. Even as I write this, I am struck by the stories I have read and been told about people from marginalised groups who had agency and power and control over their existence. It would be only telling part of the story. Parallel stories provide an antidote to the victim narrative (Table 8.2).

Table 8.2 Parallel story possibilities

If you tell the story of...	Are you also telling the story of...
Enslavement of Africans	Prominent Black campaigners for abolition, or the rebellions that were organised against enslavement? • Mary Prince • Toussaint Louverture • Frederick Douglass
Colonisation of Africa	The contribution to global knowledge of African cultures before, during and after colonisation? • The Dogon People of Mali • Influence on Cubism and Expressionism • Ethiopian empires
Colonisation of India	The early Indus Valley civilisations and their sophisticated structures? • Nalanda University as prior to Oxford • Mohenjo-Daro and early civilisation • Art of the Indus Valley
The impact of patriarchy on women	The examples of women who had power and agency? • Empress Wu Zetian • Kubaba (Ancient Sumer) • Empress Theodora

In the examples above, I am paralleling or pairing narratives so that young people can see that there is so much more to learn about when it comes to marginalised groups. If anything, it allows them to see the richness of cultures and identities beyond that of the established narrative.

About them, from them

The phrase 'Nothing about us, without us' has its origins in the politics of Central Europe, but has long since been associated with disability rights activism as a call for marginalised voices to be brought to the centre of the narrative. It has been co-opted by those advocating for racial equality, gender equality and sexuality equality over time.

It can be argued that the curriculum is not centred on these voices. Because of the patriarchal, heteronormative, ableist and racist nature of curriculum content curation in Western Europe, we do not hear often from marginalised groups. So how can we start to de-centre powerful voices using parallel stories and paired texts?

There seem to be plenty of opportunities to do this in Literature. If we take the common texts within the English Literature curriculum and deem them necessary for students to have a working knowledge of heritage texts, then we must assume that they will only hear the perspectives of those in power. To combat this, pairing texts means that we are able to flip perspectives and engage in authentic voices with lived experience (see Table 8.3 for a few examples).

Table 8.3 Paired text possibilities

Characteristic	Established text	Paired text
Disability	*Of Mice and Men*	*El Deafo*
	John Steinbeck	Cece Bell
Sexuality	*Romeo and Juliet*	*The Magic Fish*
	Shakespeare	Trung Le Nguyễn
Gender	*Great Expectations*	*The Girl of Ink and Stars*
	Charles Dickens	Kiran Milgrave Harwood
Religion	*The Crucible*	*Asha and the Spirit Bird*
	Arthur Miller	Jasbinder Bilan
Class	*An Inspector Calls*	*A Kestrel for a Knave*
	J.B. Priestley	Barry Hines
Race	*To Kill a Mockingbird*	*The Collected Poems of Langston Hughes*
	Harper Lee	Langston Hughes

Jane Eyre still inhabits a sacred space in the English Literature GCSE. My enduring memory of studying the text as a teenager was the figure of Bertha Mason, Mr Rochester's estranged ex-wife. Scholars have long argued about the racialised representation of Bertha and it not hard to see why. She is described as 'a woman tall and large, with thick and dark hair hanging down her back', who is 'Fearful and ghastly', with 'a discoloured face'. Jane recounts her fear of Bertha: 'it was a savage face. I wish I could forget the roll of red eyes and the fearful blackened inflation of linaments.' We are told that she is mad, and she came from a mad family – 'idiots and maniacs through three generations! Her mother, the Creole, was both a mad woman and a drunkard!' And even her movements are animalistic: 'a figure ran backwards and forwards. What it was, whether beast or human being, one could not, at first sight, tell: it groveled … on all fours, it snatched and growled like some strange wild animal' (Brontë, 1847).

Bertha's racial characteristics are deeply entwined with her mental state – the two are not separated. Blackness here is associated with savagery. How do we parallel this? I was struck by the justice that Jean Rhys (1966) seemed to offer Bertha in her widely acclaimed reimagining of Bertha's story in the *Wide Sargasso Sea*. She is not Bertha, but is re-given her name – Antoinette. There is a consciousness in her about the importance of names, as seen when she cries: 'Bertha is not my name, you are trying to make me into some one else, calling me by another name.'

What do we achieve by pairing these texts?

- Racial justice – we see the negatively racialised character from their viewpoint, as a whole human being.
- Empathetic consciousness – we are able to connect to the experience of the maligned character in order to empathise.
- Criticality – we are able to examine the context, the social mores, and changes to social landscape when it comes to text.

There is scope for a rich and detailed conversation. The possibilities are wide ranging (particularly at KS5). I have seen brilliant examinations of paired texts: extracts from *The Odyssey* and Madeline Miller's *Circe*; Forster's *A Passage to India* and Roy's *The God of Small Things*.

Own Voices

One of the strongest arguments for studying *Wide Sargasso Sea* is because it is, as far as possible when reconstructing a Victorian narrative, an own voice. Jean Rhys was a Creole woman with roots in Dominica.

The #OwnVoices hashtag was coined in 2015 by Corinne Duyvis and became a catch-all term for characters being written by writers who shared their characteristics. The concept of Own Voices has extended to representation elsewhere, not just in literature.

We might want to consider Own Voices in other subjects. In PSHE, how much do students engage with lived experiences as told by those who lived them? You do not need to use whole texts in order to provide access to Own Voices; you might want to consider incorporating:

- Text extracts
- Images
- Video
- Podcasts
- Interviews
- Testimonies

A wonderful way to engage in Own Voices is to invest in Lyfta, an immersive platform that allows students to explore story spaces from around the world. They 'meet' a young Black South American woman who is a musician. They meet a man in the Caribbean who is gay. The resource could function as a way of paralleling stories from around the world (www.lyfta.com, n.d.).

Finding Intersectionalities Through the Extended Project Qualification (EPQ)

I find that paralleling stories is a wonderful addition to an intersectional approach to teaching. The possibilities are endless. If we look at teaching about pregnancy and maternity, we might want to parallel the story of pregnancy and maternity for those with disabilities. This may have significant impact on real and troublesome misconceptions about disability and reproduction. On the HealthTalk website, there is a revealing set of interviews with women with disabilities, who talk about the complexities of their experiences, and some of the prejudices they faced in being pregnant and giving birth. What it highlights, alongside this, is the misconceptions that they themselves faced about their bodies, their rights and their support networks through pregnancy and childbirth.

One way that we might use a qualification to look at parallel stories is through the Extended Project Qualification (EPQ) in the UK. This qualification, the equivalent of half an A-level, allows students in further education to choose a topic and to write an academic essay on this content. There is huge potential in looking at how diverse content can be explored, research, analysed and written about.

There are banks of sample questions available, to guide students' thought processes; however, we might look at the following:

1   Why are Black women more likely to die in childbirth in the UK?

     This would pave the way to consider the experiences – the parallel stories – of white women and Black women in the NHS, using first-person narratives as well as statistics and research.

2   Should men and women be able to compete against each other in professional sports?

     This might lead to some interesting responses! We might see the profiling of athletes of differing backgrounds, body shapes and gender identification. We may see students looking at biology, at social conditioning, and at social attitudes towards gender.

3   What was the role of Mileva Maric Einstein, Albert Einstein's wife, in his scientific findings?

     This one is borrowed from a repository of questions from the Oxford Royale Academy website (2000), and it led to an immediate recognition of the potential for a parallel story (one that could be applied to other inventors and their spouses, I imagine). We could easily look at Bertha Benz and the story of her engineering feats, alongside that of her husband's.

.... **REFLECTION QUESTIONS**

- How can you plot a curriculum to include parallel stories, where some content has previously only provided a single story?
- How can you demonstrate the power of multiperspectivity in your curriculum?
- What mechanisms can you use to explore paralleling and pairing in your curriculum? Where are the opportunity areas?

9

MIGRATIONS - LINGUISTIC, CULTURAL AND PHYSICAL

Migration as a Threshold Concept

In 2019, there was a debate on migration in the History curriculum led by Labour MP Helen Hayes. Nick Gibb, the Education Secretary at the time, responded with a familiar refrain: we already have reference to migration in the History curriculum.

To a certain extent, this is true. Gibb cited exam board requirements to study:

- 'The reasons for immigration – … political, economic, social and religious.'
- 'From circa 1500: ideas of national "identity" – how we have come to define "Englishness" and "Britishness" over time.'
- 'Immigrants in England during the middle ages; their treatment by the authorities and the population generally; the extent to which they integrated.'
- 'Immigration as a political issue circa 1990 to circa 2010: the debate over a "multi-cultural society"; attitudes towards, and treatment of, political refugees and asylum seekers; the issues raised by EU "open borders".'
- 'Migration, empires and the people: circa 790 to the present day' (houseofcommons.shorthandstories.com, n.d.).

How our teaching of migration is framed is hugely important. British history tends to centre immigration to the British Isles, with particular reference to empire. I wonder what shifts need to take place in order to truly understand how much migration is part of the human condition.

Migration works in many different directions. All too often in schools, we focus on two pathways – the arrivals of newcomers to British shores and the migration of British colonisers.

Our curriculum should reflect not only the above, but migration in a broader context (Figure 9.1) and how it shaped ideas, objects, art, places and people over time.

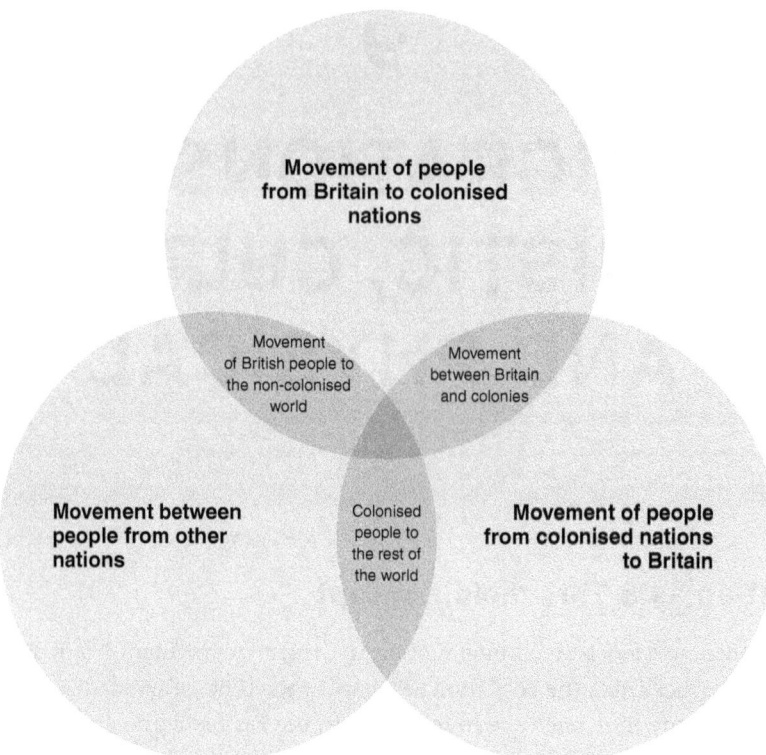

Figure 9.1   Directions of migration

It may be the case that this is more important now than ever. In 2012, Renaud Camus published *Le Grand Remplacement* (The Great Replacement), outlining the threat of 'reverse-colonisation' by Black and brown people of white Europeans. The theory gained traction amongst ethno-nationalist groups in western countries and has been used as inspiration for violent acts, such as the shooting of ten people at a market in Buffalo in 2022 and the Christchurch Mosque attacks in 2019. The perpetrators both subscribed to the idea of 'replacement' as a threat to white, western culture.

Our students may be familiar with the word 'immigrant'. They may also be familiar with the rhetoric that goes with the term in the right-wing press. Migration as a concept in the curriculum is another way to show that we have a history enriched by people who have moved locations, for work, for survival, as a result of war, famine and political upheaval.

In fact, we might consider migration to be a threshold concept for humanity. In order to understand what makes us human, we have to understand the long history of human movement. The peopling of the world was in process over 50,000 years ago. Some argue that the humans started moving in the last 100,000 years and genetic studies have reinforced this idea. Migration 8000 years ago may have brought Indo-European languages into the European continent. In the last 2000 years, the mixing of the population has become even more prevalent, for example with the movement of the Mongols bringing their DNA with them into Eastern Europe from Asia.

Scientists, anthropologists and others engaged in the study of human movement and evolution agree that there was a 'great migration' that involved early humans making the journey, often staying in warm climes and close to familiar food sources, into Asia from Africa. They outline how successive migrations saw the population of Australia, of North America and of Europe.

Teaching the Language

Language matters. The word 'immigrant' features heavily in Nick Gibbs' citation of the GCSE History curriculum. Immigrant is someone who comes in from the outside. They may be Other. Where does migrant sit in this argument? Various definitions abound on the internet: immigrant is a permanent settler, migrant is temporary. A migrant is not the same as a refugee, or asylum seeker. The world of movement is complex – but what is clear is that words create public perception, and in our schools, serve to form world-views. So how do we refer to those who have moved, for a multitude of reasons, in our curriculum?

Perhaps a starting point is to teach explicitly the language of global movement in PSHE or Geography. What are the differences in the words we use about people who move/have moved and how does that impact our perception of them (Table 9.1)?

Table 9.1 The language of movement

Term	Definition	Perception
Immigrant	Someone who settles in a different country for work or leisure.	Illegality, Other, danger
Refugee	Someone who has fled war or persecution and who has been granted permission to reside in a country not of their birth.	Misconception about status and entitlements, seen as interchangeable with asylum seeker
Asylum Seeker	Someone who is fleeing war or persecution, and is awaiting the outcome of their request to reside in a country not of their birth.	Misconceptions about status and entitlements, seen as interchangeable with refugee
Illegal immigrant	A misnomer as being undocumented in many countries does not constitute a crime. A person cannot be illegal.	Danger, invasive, Other, criminal
Alien	Used historically to describe someone who has entered a country illegally. Now considered offensive.	Foreign, dangerous, invasive, the unknown, Other
Migrant	Often used to denote someone who has moved from their country to another to seek work, or better living conditions.	Exploitative, opportunist, 'stealing our jobs'
Ex-pat	Often attributed to white Europeans who take up residence in another country.	Positive/neutral

It is hard to find alternatives to the words in our language for those who move that aren't racialised. It is interesting that cultures outside of Europe have language that denotes those who move in a neutral manner. Dereje Feyissa points out that 'Traditionally, the Hadiya [of Ethiopia] used the term *darfirma* to describe the flow of people, which is positively signified and part of the "natural order of things," not "an aberration" which needs to be controlled or managed' (Sitholé et al., 2022: 15). In Malayo-Polynesian languages, we find *merentau*, defined by Song Guan Yeoh as 'a voluntary journeying to the "outside world" for short periods of time and then, equally important, returning home to share newfound experiences, stories of adventure, novel knowledge, prestige and even wealth' (Sitholé et al., 2022: 16). Migration is part of our journey, one that takes us elsewhere and sometimes, even brings us back.

Teaching the Racialisation of Migration

Marie Tully argues that the whole concept of migration studies is flawed, as it rests on colonial thinking. Citing the work of G.K. Bhambra and A. Çaglar, she points out that 'the whole concept of migration is racialised and reproduces racist hierarchies. As Bhambra argues, "the line of mobility … is an explicitly racialised line that emerges in the context of decolonisation and the movement of darker citizens to the metropole." The movements of (wealthy) white people are clearly not labelled "migration" but rather "mobility" (Çaǧlar, 2016)' (www.imiscoe.org, n.d.).

Racial identity can come to define acceptance in an adopted country. Different countries have different informal definitions of who a migrant is. Is a white British person seen as a migrant in Germany or France? Is a North African person seen as a migrant in those places? When we talk about migration, it is important to delineate the nuances in how we see people and how our perceptions are very much filtered along race lines, and our construction of a national identity.

The Concept of Invasion

Our curriculum has always included the movement of people into Britain. My earliest memories of learning history in primary school involved learning about the invasions of the British Isles, by Angles, Saxons and Jutes. The Viking was a figure of terror, arriving to kill and displace. The language of the movement of people was not something I disputed. I grew to learn that the arrival of various groups to the British Isles may not have been a sudden displacement of 'native Britons' (I use this loosely, as I am still unclear as to who this was and what this means). In fact, what seems to be closer to the truth about these arrivals is that they consisted of some violent, invasive action and quite often a slow settlement of a region. These migrants were settling for land, economics, survival and prosperity, and they entered into negotiation and treaty in order to do so.

In the research, it is made clear that the Venerable Bede's assertion that many people arrived to the British Isles and it was 'terrible' is only partly true. The archaeological record shows there are details that supports a much longer-term movement of people: 'The graves don't tell a clear story of armed conquest. Even people with little continental DNA were buried in Anglo-Saxon fashion, suggesting they willingly adopted the new culture. And the DNA shows both women and men immigrated. The team also found many individuals had a mixture of DNA from continental Europe and eastern Great Britain, suggesting intermarriage and integration lasted for centuries' (www.science.org, n.d.).

So even our earliest narratives in the UK about the invasions of the British Isles need to have more nuance.

How Long Have You Been Here?

One of the biggest misconceptions about migration is that society has been flooded with new arrivals from the middle of the 20th century onwards and that British culture has been negatively affected as a result. Students are not often afforded the opportunity to learn that people have arrived on British shores for centuries, for multitudes of reasons.

The history of Black presence in Britain often starts in the Tudor period, and yet, there is evidence of Black presence from significantly earlier periods. In the 3rd century AD, a legion of Moors was stationed at Hadrian's Wall and this group, the 'Aurelian Moors', were known to have settled and had families in Britain whilst defending the Roman Empire's northern borders. They may have been recruited from the Berber people of Mauritania, what is now Morocco and Algeria. Evidence of sub-Saharan African presence also exists earlier than this. The Ivory Bangle Lady was discovered in York in 1901, with riches that denote her status. In 1241, we see the first drawing of a Black Briton in the Domesday Book. The Tudor period brings, as Miranda Kaufmann points out, musicians, soldiers, interpreters and more (Kaufmann, 2018). By the time we hit the 1760s, there are thought to be at least 20,000 Black people in Britain, with the majority concentrated in London.

There is a similar story with people of South East Asian origin. Rozina Visram provides a detailed look at the presence of South East Asian populations in Britain, the earliest of whom she states are the 17th-century lascars, or sailors, who travelled on trading ships as employees but were often left to fend for themselves in Britain on arrival, with no fare to go back home. These lascars formed communities, settled and had families as a result of British colonial activity. This is neatly summarised in Ambalavaner Sivananda's aphorism: 'We are here because you were there' (Institute of Race Relations, n.d.).

There are references to South Asian communities and figures peppered throughout the historical record.

Migration and Impact on Culture

The movement of people inevitably impacts on culture in places. It stands to reason that cultural exchange is the result of travel and migration. In teaching Dance, for example, we might choose to look at Morris Dancing as a British form and reference the name possibly originating from the term 'Moorish' dancing, even though the form bears little resemblance to dance enacted in North Africa. It is likely, researchers say, that some aspects of the dance may have been developed through centuries of cultural exchange between North Africa and Europe.

We are introduced to new ideas and customs through our interaction with migrants and their cultures. Something as innocuous as hair washing can highlight how migrants bring cultural practices that become our everyday life. Shampooing as a concept is said to have originated in Indus Valley civilisations. The European use of soap and water was superseded by shampoo thanks to Sake Dean Mohamed, a migrant from South East Asia who opened a Turkish-style bath in Brighton in which he offered 'shampoo' services. It was taken on commercially by white, Western European people as a result. Perhaps a sequence of learning on personal hygiene could include this information.

Art is a cultural conversation, with artistic movements drawing on earlier and more global artistic endeavours. The Art Deco movement in particular is interesting, drawing on emerging fascination with Egyptian history and culture as a result of Howard Carter's excavation of the tomb of Tutankhamen. Art Deco also saw the use of African textiles and figures, as exemplified by Sigmund Pollitzer's panel in 1933. This is less migration-based, but an indicator that art does not see geographical boundaries when it makes the leap from one continent to another. Artists cross geographical boundaries and enrich the art of the nation they have adopted: look at the work of Sir Anish Kapoor, or Dame Zaha Hadid, or indeed, Marc Chagall.

There are possibilities in exploring this idea, for example:

- Teaching about the origins of the guitar as being from the European lute and the Arabic Oud in Music lessons.
- Drawing on cultural influences in architecture in DT lessons.
- Looking at global representations of the female body in Art (and the feminist campaigns against museums in the 1970s/1980s).
- Tracing the travels of spice in Food lessons.

Using Language to Expand Boundaries

Using language to show the impact of migration is also an opportunity to find connection. Etymology is a complex field, but scholars working on the development of words over time and place make some extraordinary connections that we often fail to signpost in our education systems. Words are developed and move over space and time.

Take the names of numbers, as a first example. The origins of 'two' as a word can be traced back to the Proto-Hellenic *dúwō*, or similarly, the Proto-Italic *duō*, which brings us to the *deux*, *dos* and *due* of the European world. It can also be traced to the Proto-Germanic *twai*, which takes a more direct path to our *two* via the Old English *twā*. What's missing here is the information that all of these routes come from the Proto-Indo-European *dwóh*, which connects all of the variations given in this paragraph, but also the roads leading to the Punjabi *do*, the Romani *duy*, the Rohingya *dui* and the Kurdish *du*. Our words are all related.

Languages themselves are impacted by migration. If we look at variation in French as a language between Francophone countries, we can see the sometimes subtle changes that are made in movement. Quebecois French is similar to, but not the same as, French in France. Before I knew better, I would have said my home language is Gujarati; however I have learned since that it is far removed from the language of the Gujarat, in that it is infused with Swahili, as my parents were East-African Asian. Their migration shifted their language and I inherited a different form of it. Language teachers might not see the significance of mentioning this, but validating migration-led adaptations to language allows young people to see language not as a fixed monolith, but as something that is ever-shifting.

Mathematical Language and Migration

If we look at the word 'algebra', are we making it clear where this word came from? It is widely believed that it stems from *al-jabr*, an Arabic word meaning 'the reunion of broken parts'. Or is it made common knowledge that algebra has travelled far and wide – from the rhetorical algebra of the Babylonians, to the syncopated algebra of the Diophantus Arithmetica, to the symbolic algebra of Islamic mathematicians that brought us to Cartesian Geometry. What about the 'tri-' in triangle? Why does it evoke three in both Eastern and Western cultures?

I have already spoken about the origins of zero in *A Little Guide for Teachers: Diversity in Schools* (Kara, 2020: 42). A reminder:

> It seems vitally important to understand the global contribution to the development of zero. Without zero, we would not be living in our digital age – one that is predicated on the marked, binary existence of something and nothing. Even the language of zero creates cultural connection; the earliest word is 'sunya' (Sanskrit), Arabian scholars called it 'sifr', Fibonacci called it 'zephyrum', Italians used 'zefiro' and it transcribed into English as zero in 1598.

Numbers themselves are the result of cross-cultural study, travel and migration. Our number system, what we call Arabic numerals, originate in the Brahmi scripts of India, move into their next incarnation in Hindu numerals with small changes, then they are taken on by the Arabian world, before landing on European shores. They don't magically migrate themselves, they are disseminated through cross-cultural study, notably in this case by Fibonacci, who interacted with Hindu and Arabic scholars in his time as a customs official in what is now modern day Bejaïa in Algeria. On publishing his seminal work, *Liber Abaci* (1202), he is said to have been the connection between the European mathematical world and the older Middle East and India.

Migration and Food

Food items and dishes are cultural artefacts, bringing with them the history of their places of origin. Migration has played a huge role in the development of British cuisine. Our very tastes have been shaped by those who arrived here as migrants. In 'Immigration and the Making of British Food', Professor Panikos Panayi outlines the myriad ways in which food items and dishes we would consider to be exceedingly British came to be here. The first coffee houses were set up by migrants such as Pasqua Rosee. Italian migrants brought us ice cream, setting up community and business in Clerkenwell. Fish and chips, that quintessential British dish, has Jewish origins and Italians were instrumental in developing fish and chips into established British cuisine (Panayi, 2020).

Food items have a fascinating history. When we teach students about food items, either in the primary phase or as part of the Food curriculum in DT, we have the opportunity to handle misconceptions, as well as enrich our students' understanding of where food comes from and how it ties in with culture, climate and migration – and colonisation. Potatoes were domesticated in Peru and arrived on European shores as a result of Spanish sailors returning from their colonial travels. Rice was cultivated in China originally, travelling through India and the Middle East before landing in Europe from North Africa. Tea, or chai, has an equally long journey. The origins of the two names is a teaching point in itself: it is tea over the sea, and cha over the land. Why? Because 'cha' is Sinitic and was transported as such via the Silk Road, and the Min Nan version of tea, 'te', is a coastally located term and spread to Europe via the Dutch using naval routes.

Another item that has a history, a more troubled history, is sugar. Most of us will be aware of the history of sugar. I recall being taught that Elizabethans ate so much sugar that their teeth turned black, and that it was a mark of wealth to have blackened teeth because it meant you could afford sugar, a pricey and extravagant delight. No one told me who was used to make the sugar. While I now know that sugar arrived in Britain as early as the 11th century, via Portuguese exploration, it was the Dutch and British who transformed sugar cultivation through enslavement. Sugar is intrinsically linked with mass enslavement and death. Sweet as it might be, there has been a heavy price to pay for enslaved people who were transported through the Middle Passage.

Physical Migrations

It is important to place in context the impact of physical migrations on society, and to frame them positively. We have become more aware of physical migrations in recent history due to news coverage on the arrival and legacy of the Windrush generation. In teaching about the *Empire Windrush*, we can look closely at the impact those arrivals had on British society – the fact that they were needed to rebuild Britain after the Second World War. What is often not studied is the effect of migration on, for example, music and culture: the British music scene, very much centred on swing and dance bands, was enhanced by infusions of jazz, reggae, calypso, ska and so on.

We can tell the story of the arrival of the Windrush generation, but ensure that there is a positive focus. It might be the case that we look at the significant figures of the Windrush generation, such as Diane Abbott or Bernie Grant. We can look at the contribution of Windrush to the newly-formed NHS. It is an exercise of celebration. Of course, there is also a need to look at the lasting problem of compensation for Windrush migrants.

The story of new arrivals and how they were treated has been spotlighted by the Channel 4 documentary series *Defiance*. In this three-part show, the documentary makers recount the racism that was faced by South Asian communities in West London and East London, and how resistance to fascists manifested in those communities. The physical migrations of the 20th century to Britain from South Asian communities are partially known, but not widely understood or celebrated.

But we see the cultural impact of this migration daily – in our food, in our politics, in our music. One such migration is particularly pertinent to my own life. My family arrived in the UK in the 1970s as a result of political turmoil in East Africa. The story of the Ugandan refugees fleeing from Idi Amin's dictatorship is a seminal migration tale; it is one that sees cultural change in many British cities. I did not know, for example, that on arrival, my family were placed in a resettlement camp. I did not know the political context – related to colonialism – of my family's forced movement. I did not know what to call them – refugees, subjects, foreigners? The language was not taught because the story was not told.

Perhaps there is a reluctance to tell the story of some migrations because they place British colonialism as a troublesome engagement. We have not yet reached a time when we can talk about the impact of empire, even on Britain itself, without stirring up nationalism and defensiveness.

In South Africa, Nelson Mandela and his peers took on the mammoth task of establish the Truth and Reconciliation Commission, to reconcile the violence and oppression of Apartheid. The Promotion of National Unity and Reconciliation Act 34 of 1995 stipulated the following:

> Since the Constitution of the Republic of South Africa, 1993 (Act 200 of 1993), provides a historic bridge between the past of a deeply divided society characterized by strife, conflict, untold suffering and injustice, and a future founded on the recognition of human rights, democracy and peaceful co-existence for all South Africans, irrespective of colour, race, class, belief or sex;

> And since it is deemed necessary to establish the truth in relation to past events as well as the motives for and circumstances in which gross violations of human rights have occurred, and to make the findings known in order to prevent a repetition of such acts in future;

> And since the Constitution states that the pursuit of national unity, the well-being of all South African citizens and peace require reconciliation between the people of South Africa and the reconstruction of society;

> And since the Constitution states that there is a need for understanding but not for vengeance, a need for reparation but not for retaliation, a need for ubuntu but not for victimization; …

I am struck by the language of this law. It is based on reconstruction, on the principles of Ubuntu (the African principle of humanity towards others) and on establishing truth a central part of that process.

How then do we talk about the impact of Partition on migration (regionally, as well as internationally)? How do we apply these principles to British politicking overseas as part of imperial rule, and the way in which it affected people's movement, forced or otherwise?

Maybe it is time to look for truth and reconciliation when we teach about migration. Perhaps it would lead to better conversations about why people move and the impact they have, and importantly, how they felt and still feel today about moving from their homes to establish lives in Britain.

REFLECTION QUESTIONS

- How does your subject lend itself to discussion of migration?
- What are the contributions of migrants to the knowledge in your subject?
- How does migration form a thread through your curriculum?
- How do you highlight the positive stories of migrants in your subject?

10

ROLE MODELS

Growing up as an Asian girl in Leicester, I went to a school that was 90% Asian. The community was predominantly Asian but none of my teachers were Asian, in primary school at least. There was little reference to Asian women as role models. In secondary school I met the first Asian teachers I had ever seen. They weren't school leaders but at least they were visible as members of staff in the system. I have no recollection of any teaching that mentioned Asian women. To me Asian women were the women I saw in my community, predominantly mothers – those who worked alongside their husbands in small businesses. So my perception of Asian women was that they existed only in the domestic sphere. I had no reference points for Asian women as scientists or writers, or business owners or academics.

When I speak to my Asian friends now it is clear that the result of this absence of role models led to anxiety and confusion for us. What were we to be? The reality was that we were subject to our parents' understanding of our futures and we had little else to pin our hopes and dreams upon. I now wonder whether learning about Indian princesses who were suffragettes would have made an impact on me as a child or influenced the kind of subjects that I chose to study. I simply wasn't aware of what Asian women could be capable of.

For some of our children, even though time has moved on and people of colour are more visible in society and their contributions have been acknowledged, they are still lacking in role models. One particular problem that has been identified is a lack of *British* role models of colour. The heroes of recent culture tend to be American, and it has been identified that British children in particular have very little understanding of the role models that exist within our own culture.

This is not just an anecdote. The field of research on role modelling is rich with examples of how, given the right conditions, people from marginalised groups can feel a sense of belonging through seeing successful role models of their own identity. Nilanjana Dasgupta's Stereotype Inoculation Model outlines the need for, and the effects of, having role models who function as 'social vaccines' against a lack of belonging. In her work, she explains: 'what *feels* like a free choice to pursue one life path or "possible self" over another is often constrained by subtle cues in achievement environments that signal who naturally belongs there and is most likely to succeed and who else is a dubious fit' (Dasgupta, 2011: 231). Her work is important when we consider how students see themselves in school and in the curriculum. The effect of not seeing oneself in the curriculum may have an impact on progress and attainment, attendance and wellbeing. Dasgupta cites bodies of research on this impact when she explains how 'stereotype threat and social identity threat are known to undermine performance in domains where one's group is negatively stereotyped and one's belonging uncertain; over time, weak performance reduces self-confidence in one's ability (or self-efficacy) and leads individuals to withdraw from the domain'.

Is this just a call for more people to be included in the curriculum, from different backgrounds? Partially, yes. In doing this, we expand awareness of role models from different fields, and we build a more accurate representation of the world. In practice, there are some considerations to be explored.

To Display or not to Display?

It is tempting to address the need for role models by creating static displays of diverse people on the walls of our classrooms, or in our corridors. It feels concrete and reassuring. Anyone looking will see that we know about diverse role models. Except, it is pretty surface in its scope if we confine diverse role models to the walls of our environment. Their place is in the curriculum, in the meat of the lesson, in the spread of pastoral activities and in the conversations that take place in the rooms we work in. I call the displays Shrines to LGBTQ+ People[1] in the corners of our room.

In the absence of any other diversity in your school's environment, displays can be useful. They can flag up hidden figures and spark curiosity in our students. They say 'we know that there are people out there who look like you, have bodies like you and have religion like you'. The key here is to consider what the balance of representation is. If you have displays that feature significant Western European men, then there is a responsibility to demonstrate that other people exist and have value in our world, in the domain of our subjects, in their fields of endeavour.

Intersectionality of Significant Figures

Are all your role models from one culture? Are they all men? Are they all able-bodied? It strikes me that often in our quest to diversify the curriculum, we insert figures that are only one step removed from the established power base. If we include women at all as role models, then it is likely that they will be white women. When we evaluate the curriculum, we often congratulate ourselves for adding in women, forgetting to check sometimes whether women of all cultures, sexualities, religions and abilities are represented.

One significant role model in literature is James Baldwin. Baldwin's work is situated in the Civil Rights Movement in the US and incorporates his identity as a Black man

---

[1] You can replace this with any marginalised characteristic. It still works.

whose sexuality (although undefined by Baldwin himself) was important enough to surface in his books. Baldwin's work may not be Key Stage 3, or Key Stage 4 standard fare, but he is a figure to feature at Key Stage 5 in English Literature, or perhaps even in History modules on civil rights.

If we consider athletes with disabilities, we may struggle to name significant figures to reference in PE who are female, and certainly struggle to name global majority athletes with disabilities. We may know Ellie Simmonds as a result of her appearance in *Strictly Come Dancing*. Or we may know Dame Tanni Grey-Thompson, who has had a long and illustrious career as a sportsperson, TV presenter and now life peeress. She might appear in the curriculum as someone who lives with spina bifida, or we may refer to her role as a life peeress when explaining the political system of the UK.

The Algorithm Effect

At times, we allocate responsibility for the finding of role models to our young people, through research projects and assemblies. There they are, our students, using search engines to find famous geographers. In Safiya Umoja Noble's fascinating book on the racialised and misogynistic nature of search engines, *Algorithms of Oppression: How Search Engines Reinforce Racism* (2018), we see that there are fundamental issues with the way in which information is curated on the internet. In the book, Noble questions what happens when you use the search term 'Black girls' on Google. She points out that searches for whiteness do not generate the same racist and misogynistic content.

If our students type in 'famous geographers', who are they likely to see? My own search is a microcosm of the problem. Of the first 13 images returned, they are predominantly white men, one of whom is Prince William. What do students absorb through this algorithm? This is what a geographer looks like. Type in 'famous engineers UK' and it is mostly white men, apart from a surprise appearance by Hedy Lamarr, not a surprise because she was *not* an engineer and inventor, but because she was Austrian-American. What about 'famous athletes UK?' We have Lewis Hamilton, Mo Farah, Dina Asher-Smith, Jessica Ennis. Black is acceptable in sport.

The proactive countering of this effect lies in careful curation of the role models that we want our young people to see. If left to chance, and indeed, the algorithm, then perhaps we will only perpetuate bias.

The Fallout

Not everyone is keen on schools choosing diverse role models. In 2021, successful headteacher of Howden Junior School, Lee Hill, faced significant public backlash when staff made the choice to modernise the school's house names. Staff choose to replace Walter Raleigh and Francis Drake with modern figures such as Greta Thunberg and Marcus Rashford. This was done in recognition of the problematic nature of the original figures as flagged by a concerned ex-pupil; Raleigh was a coloniser who played a part in the subjugation and murder of indigenous peoples. Drake was known to be an enslaver, possibly even one of the first in British history. It is understandable that a school might want to distance themselves from figures who are associated with such horrors. Unfortunately, Piers Morgan caught hold of the story and Lee Hill faced hideous amounts of abuse on social media, as he had been deemed by *The Sun* and other papers as 'Britain's "Wokest" Headmaster' (Hammond and Moyes, 2021).

Stories like this inevitably serve to put teachers off making changes in school, in the curriculum or elsewhere, that reflect modern sensitivities and modern concerns. When we make changes, our responsibility is to the education of our students. We show them that people can be questioned, figures that used to be worshipped can be problematic and that our relationship with the past is ever changing. A good curriculum will put disciplinary questions into the discussion about people and their long-cultivated image. It will encourage enquiry and reflection.

Dead White Men

Brandon Hogan explains in his blog for the American Philosophical Association that he became aware of the controversies associated with some of the dead white men in the philosophy curriculum. In it, he explores Hegel and the racism that was espoused by Hegel in *The Philosophy of History*. He cites Hegel as saying:

> At this point [in the story of world history] we leave Africa, not to mention it again. For it is no historical part of the world; it has no movement or development to exhibit. Historical movements in it – that is in its Northern part – belong to the Asiatic or European World. ... What we properly understand by Africa, is the unhistorical, undeveloped spirit, still involved in the conditions of mere nature, and which had to be presented here only as on the threshold of the world's history. Having eliminated this introductory element, we find ourselves for the first time on the real theater of history. It is in the Caucasian race that spirit first reaches absolute unity with itself. (in Hogan, 2022)

Hogan admits that it is nearly impossible to avoid referencing and studying dead white men, even though some have held abhorrent views. For the teacher, this is also true. What is important here is the need for discernment and for questioning of how we present figures such as Hume or Hegel, and how to show young people the complexity of venerated figures. So, we introduce them, we reference their contributions to the field of study, and ensure that we make clear their personal views (and how this may have impacted on their work). It is an act of critical thinking to be able to hold more than one view of people and ideas. It is only when we present a problematic figure uncritically that we do our young people a disservice.

One of the biggest critics of this approach was Harold Bloom. In *The Western Canon*, Bloom codified the figures in literature that he deemed to exemplify the best of Western European thinking. The list included: Shakespeare, Dante Alighieri, Chaucer, Milton, Wordsworth, Johnson, Austen, Dickens, Dickinson, Whitman, Woolf, Kafka and Neruda. At least there were some women on his list. Bloom's perspective on the canon as he defined it was pretty clear. He actively criticised what he termed 'a school of resentment', one in which critics sought to expand the boundaries of their canon to include racial diversity and more women, at the expense of 'literary merit'. He was interviewed by the *Paris Review* in 1991, where he elaborated, and it makes for eye-opening reading (Weiss, 1991).

This perspective is not one confined to the past. In the most recent review of English by Ofsted, we see the following statement: 'in a significant number of schools, texts for study in English are not always chosen for their literary merit. Instead, they cover aspects of personal, social and health education, and current affairs. This gives pupils a disjointed experience of literature, because the concepts, such as narrative voice, are not well connected across the text choices to support pupils to deepen their understanding. While pupils can learn from all books, English curriculums should give careful consideration to texts of literary merit that would support pupils in their understanding of English now and in the future. Other books should form an essential part of the wider curriculum or reading for pleasure' (Ofsted, 2024).

Time may have moved on, but the Western canonical lens lives on.

Problematic Figures

One only needs to look at recent events in the United Kingdom to see that choosing who we commemorate, celebrate and laud as a role model is thorny. Many of our schools are named after figures who, in a modern context, might be seen as controversial. In Bristol, the toppling of Edward Colston's statue as part of a protest against his activities as an enslaver triggered discussions as to whether schools and other institutions named after him should be renamed. Of course, the hand wringing about this was inevitable. Should we rename organisations named after Columbus, or even Churchill in light of our understanding of colonisation and racism? Churchill is politically deified, and yet we know, as Priyamvada Gopal (2021) points out, that 'Churchill is on record as praising "Aryan stock" and insisting it was right for "a stronger race, a higher-grade race" to take the place of indigenous peoples ... Churchill banned interracial boxing matches so white fighters would not be seen losing to black ones. He insisted that Britain and the US shared "Anglo-Saxon superiority". He described anticolonial campaigners as "savages armed with ideas".'

In the science curriculum, one of the few named scientists is Carl Linnaeus. He is not cited as one of the progenitors of race science, but instead at KS2 as the father of classification of living things. A role model, as such. But his work, alongside the work of Blumenbach and others, forms the basis of racial narratives that echo through the generations. Should he be so present in the curriculum? And if so, when do we teach children that he may have formulated classification of living things, but that he also formulated thoughts such as those shown in Table 10.1.

Table 10.1 Linnaeus's classification of races

Species	Colour and Physique	Physical Appearance	Nature	Body and adornment
Homo Americanus	Red, choleric and straight	Straight, black, thick hair; gaping nostrils; [freckled] face; beardless chin	Unyielding, cheerful, free	Paints himself in a maze of red lines
Homo Europaeus	White, sanguine, muscular	Plenty of yellow hair; blue eyes	Light, wise, inventors	Protected by tight clothing
Homo Asiaticus	Sallow, melancholic, stiff	Blackish hair, dark eyes	Stern, haughty, greedy	Protected by loose garments
Homo Africanus	Black, phlegmatic, lazy	Dark hair, twisting braids; silky skin; flat nose; swollen lips; elongated labia; breasts lactating	Sly, sluggish, neglectful	Anoints himself with fat

Linnaeus is not going anywhere, but herein lies the responsibility to inform students not just of his work on classification of living things, but in the categorisation of human beings into races and how we still deal with the racial ideas that stem from his work.

Modern Role Models and the Danger of not Knowing

Choosing modern role models can be risky. At university, I was fascinated by international politics, as were many of my peers. Aung Sang Suu Kyi was held up as a rebel leader, someone to be admired for her efforts to liberate Myanmar. There was even talk of naming one of the students' union bars after her. She was awarded the Nobel Peace Prize in 1991, even as she sat under house arrest. An inspiring person, surely? And yet, her recent record has given many pause for thought on her politics and her stance on religion, as her treatment of Rohingya Muslims has been seen as potentially genocidal.

Significant figures who are still alive, still have room to err. Does that mean we cannot hold them as role models? No, but it does mean that we must exercise due diligence and ensure that we are willing to have conversations about changes to their status in our society. We must be willing to remove them from our curriculum and school structures, if we learn that they do not represent an equitable society.

LGBTQ+ Role Models

One common narrative around LGBTQ+ figures in our curriculum is that they are subject to oppression and that is why they should be studied. There is little focus on the achievements of LGBTQ+ people who not only survive a homophobic society, but thrive in it. A classic example is teaching about Alan Turing as a significant wartime figure and central protagonist within the IT curriculum. Turing was a mathematician and computer scientist famous for his work supporting the development of the Enigma machine that helped to crack German code during the Second World War. Turing was also prosecuted for homosexual acts in 1952 and was forced to undergo chemical castration. Turing was found dead in 1954, apparently from cyanide poisoning. The fact that a half eaten apple was found next to him has led to some believing that the Turing inspired the Apple logo. In displays in schools he will often be lauded as evidence that LGBTQ+ figures are present in the curriculum, but it is often forgotten that his is a tragic tale, despite the fact that Queen Elizabeth II pardoned him posthumously.

In fact, research shows that LGBTQ+ figures and suicide are intrinsically linked within our cultural context. Within the gay community, it is seen as a source of amusement and despair that LGBTQ+ figures are allowed to be present in the texts and in the TV shows that we watch, as long as they are linked with death in some way. The literary community has been aware of this trope for many years now. It is no surprise that you can look up 'dead lesbian syndrome' and find article after article on how lesbians can be present as long as they are made unhappy. This reinforces the idea that what is perceived as deviance must be corrected in some way, shape or form within our stories. Haley Hulan (2017: 17) calls this phenomenon 'Bury Your Gays' and defines it as a trope featuring 'a same-gender couple and with one of the lovers dying and the other realizing they were never actually gay, often running into the arms of a heterosexual partner. This trope was originally used as a way for gay authors to write about gay characters without coming under fire for breaking laws and social mandates against the "endorsement" of homosexuality.'

This is why it's so important to present LGBT figures as living, successful contributors to our society. If we are to present LGBT people as fully rounded, we must balance our content on Alan Turing with content that reflects those who made significant contributions and are not defined by their deaths.

Victims and Agency

Presenting role models from underrepresented groups can often lead us into the same trap, time and time again – that we only ever showcase diverse figures in light of their oppression, with little reference to their agency, their innovation and their achievements.

Black history is particularly prone to being taught like this. In the common narrative, enslavement is enacted and then 'solved' by white British men, such as William Wilberforce. We spend little time examining the agency or action of Black abolitionists such as Harriet Tubman, Fredrick Douglass or Mary Prince.

Mary Prince is a significant figure in British history, as she was the first Black woman to write and publish her autobiography in England. Her work may have had significant impact on solidifying the anti-slavery movement in the years before the Slavery

Abolition Act of 1833. The first Black man to write and publish his autobiography was Ottobah Cugoano in 1787, and he was one of the first Black abolitionists to publicly decry enslavement in England and demand abolition.

Even when we look at those who were victims of the British Empire, we have the responsibility to examine how resistance, organisation and campaigning were enacted. I often recount the history of the Rani of Jhansi. She is a fascinating example of resistance and there is a detailed account of her life by Harleen Singh (2016).

In 1828, Marnikarna Tambe was born in Varanasi, where girls were afforded an education that included shooting, fencing and horsemanship (all of which would prove handy later on in life). She married the 5th Maharajah of Jhansi and became known as Lakshmibai, in honour of the goddess Lakshmi. She adopted the Maharajah's cousin's son just before her husband's untimely death. Despite a request to the British that Jhansi remain untouched, it was quickly made apparent that the land was to be annexed in the absence of a legitimate male heir. The Rani protested, but the land was seized.

When the Indian Rebellion started in 1857, the Rani resumed her leadership of Jhansi and raised an army of both men and women, to whom she gave military training. It is said that she may have modelled this training by steeplechasing and weightlifting before breakfast!

Her rebellion was not successful ultimately. The British bombarded the fort and the casualties were enormous. All civilians were massacred in 1858 in Jhansi. The Rani fled with her son tied to her back, but was fatally wounded.

What a woman. She is revered as a national heroine in parts of India, immortalised in song and film and commemorated by statues. Yet she is a figure we do not hear about. We know who Joan of Arc is, but the Rani of Jhansi, the Indian Joan of Arc, is rarely featured in the curriculum anywhere.

Who can You Bring to the Table?

There is a wealth of information out there speculating on the sexualities of famous historical figures. It is worth knowing that these speculations exist, perhaps, if anything, it allows us to see that sexuality has always been a source of speculation and intrigue. Figures such as Leonardo Da Vinci have been cited as gay (inasmuch as we can use the modern terminology to describe someone in a completely different time and context), with Freud himself embarking on a study that looked at Da Vinci's possibly homosexual acts and feelings.

Monarchs, as subject as they are to political manoeuvres through the historical record, have been cited as gay. Not just James I, whose 'relationships' with George Villiers and Robert Carr have long been scrubbed from record, but also Richard I with his alleged relationship with Phillip II of France.

With this in mind, it is important to remind ourselves to focus on the title of this chapter – role models. As much as I would love to see a young person seeing themselves in James I, it is less likely than if we had someone centred in the curriculum who is more historically recent, and relevant.

Role models do not have to sit in history. At a school I worked in, there was a weekly careers/aspiration assembly. Our students 'met' all sorts of people working in the local area from all different backgrounds. Black engineers, female, Muslim biochemists, sports people with disabilities. It was joyous. There was never a sense that a role model had to look a certain way, or to fit into a mould. We actively wanted to show our students that 'being' in this world was an opportunity – and look, lots of people exist like you out there in the world of work.

In light of the complexity of choosing role models for your subject, I can only suggest some simple checks and balances to ensure that we are spotlighting significant figures with accuracy. This means we have to do meaningful research and ask ourselves the important questions.

REFLECTION QUESTIONS

- Why are they significant in my subject?
- Are they the only figure I can choose to exemplify my subject?
- Aside from their subject-based significance, are they famous for anything else (particularly problematic viewpoints)?
- Can I do without them?
- If I do include them, how can I ensure that they are presented through a critical lens?

11

COUNTERING DOMINANT NARRATIVES

What is a dominant narrative? It is, put simply, a common belief held socially and within the consciousness of our society that may not be accurate. Certainly, we may not always be aware that we are influenced by, or hold value in these dominant narratives. First comes recognition of what these dominant narratives are, and then we are bound to provide 'counter-narratives'. Bamberg and Andrews (2004) explore the ways in which 'master narratives' are intrinsically linked to our positioning of ourselves and others in society, and how we need counter-narratives to tackle misconstructions of our world. In this chapter, I will look at some common 'master narratives' and consider how we can provide the counter-narratives for them.

Dominant Narrative: Disability is Undesirable

Think about how you encountered disability for the first time. For some, this will be through first-hand experience, either through a family member who has a disability, or through personal, own body experience. For those who do not have those experiences, disability is outside of a day-to-day understanding. We grow up (sometimes) seeing disability as something that happens or has happened to other people. For these people, disability is experienced through books and through the media.

In *Disabling Imagery and the Media: An Exploration of the Principles for Media Representations of Disabled People*, Colin Barnes (1992) provides a comprehensive overview of the harmful tropes associated with disability in the media. For quick reference, the list is as follows, but the research paper is well worth a proper read:

- The Disabled Person as Pitiable and Pathetic
- The Disabled Person as an Object of Violence
- The Disabled Person as Sinister and Evil

- The Disabled Person as Atmosphere or Curio
- The Disabled Person as Super Cripple
- The Disabled Person as an Object of Ridicule
- The Disabled Person as Their Own Worst and Only Enemy
- The Disabled Person as Burden
- The Disabled Person as Sexually Abnormal
- The Disabled Person as Incapable of Participating Fully in Community Life
- The Disabled Person as Normal

I encountered disability through books, film and TV as a child. I have early recollections of the piteous story of the Elephant Man, of being frightened by the sinister Captain Hook, and now that I think about it, reading *The Secret Garden* and somehow being convinced that Colin could just get better if he engaged with the physically fit Dickson and Mary. In Colin lie many harmful tropes. I went on to study representations of disability in 19th-century children's literature as part of my Masters in English. This was transformational for me, in that I was able to see how we become inured to the negative representation of groups of people because those representations are embedded in our culture. It was especially enlightening to learn about the link between public health and perceptions of nationhood. The mid-19th century saw the rise of 'Muscular Christianity', a movement linking physical fitness to morality. In this, we see also that a healthy population is necessary for the economy (we need a supply of physically able workers), and the leaders of our nations have to be perceived as healthy or there is perceived to be corruption at the top. In Diana Mulock Craik's *The Little Lame Prince and His Travelling Cloak* (1875), we see Prince Dolor banished to a tower due to his physical disability; his healthy cousin is placed on the throne in his stead.

One of the contradictions of encountering disability lies in the layering of information about disability over time. Children absorb their social environment, are coded with messages about disability such as Barnes's list and yet, expected to empathise with people with disabilities – to say the right things about fairness and equality when they are at school. There is no objection to this latter circumstance, of course, but this may create a superficial understanding of disability, which, in turn, perpetuates the lack of equity in our society for people with disabilities.

People with disabilities are more likely to experience bullying, less likely to be employed, more likely to experience hate crimes, less likely to have access to adequate resources and more likely to die younger than their counterparts without a disability.

Countering Narratives

- Learn about the nuances of disability.
- Actively counter stereotypes of disability (and how historical views have formed these stereotypes).
- Create encounters with disability through texts and biographies.
- Celebrate role models with disabilities in the present and past (ensuring that you are considering the intersections with disability).

Dominant Narrative: Empire was a Positive Endeavour

As I grew up in modern Britain, I declared myself to be 'a child of Empire'. I had no other way of defining myself, I thought, since my parents had been – in Africa and in India before that – colonial subjects. Looking back, I am alarmed to remember this label I made for myself. What had I learned about the British Empire growing up? From my parents, little other than the fact they had British passports. From school, the idea that the British Empire was a civilising force.

At no point in my education did we discuss the realities of Empire for its colonial subjects. Later on, in teaching, I saw history teachers ask students to complete the 'balance sheet' of Empire; in what ways, they asked, was Empire beneficial to colonial subjects and to Britain? And in what ways detrimental?

The balance sheet task always seemed so *balanced*. As an adult, with an accumulated and thorough knowledge of the cruelty and exploitation of the British Empire, I often wondered why we used this balance sheet approach. It became more and more acceptable to talk about the negatives of the Empire – as long as we balanced those with the supposed mitigating factors of colonialism.

Why don't we talk about the Rwandan genocide that way? It would be, as you can imagine, highly inappropriate to create a balance sheet of actions in Rwanda. Similarly with the Holocaust – it would cause outrage to absolve Nazis of their crimes by providing mitigating circumstances. It would be simply unacceptable.

Some factors to consider: the Indian economist Utsa Patnaik, Professor Emerita at the Centre for Economic Studies and Planning at Jawaharlal Nehru University in New Delhi, estimates in her research that 'Over roughly 200 years, the East India Company and the British Raj siphoned out at least £9.2 trillion (or $44.6 trillion; since the exchange rate was $4.8 per pound sterling during much of the colonial period)' (Patnaik and Patnaik, 2021). This 'drain of wealth' meant that India was not able to develop economically or technologically at the same rate as Japan, for instance, in the 1870s. The economic impact of Empire was huge.

But the social and personal impact was worse. What I did not know growing up was the extent to which the British Empire enacted physical violence upon its subjects. I was not taught about the subjugation of Indians. I heard the term 'Indian Mutiny' and focused on the mutiny aspect of it; in the terminology lay the blame. I did not know the number of Indian dead. Some historians place the figure of deaths of Indians in reprisal for the 'rebellion' at 100,000. Other historians, such as Amaresh Misra, place the number much higher. Misra 'argues that there was an "untold holocaust" which caused the deaths of almost 10 million people over 10 years beginning in 1857' (Misra 2007, cited in Ramesh, 2007).

The question of how to teach about the British Empire is always present. In this, as teachers, we are navigating both facts and feelings, not just our own, but those of our students, their families, our colleagues and the prevailing ideas of our times. It is no wonder, then, that we often resort to the balance sheet method of analysing the impact of Empire. We ask our students to identify and analyse the pros and cons of Empire, something that the Equalities Minister in the UK in 2022 may have missed when she called for there to be a recognition that 'There were terrible things that happened during the British Empire, there were other good things that happened, and we need to tell both sides of the story' (Alibhai, 2022). Kemi Badenoch cites her own education on the British Empire as the reason why she takes, in her words, such a nuanced approach. This is a fascinating glimpse into how colonial history works: a nation that was colonised presenting itself (at least in this case) as a beneficiary of Empire's bounty, with a nod to some terrible things. It is worth noting here that Nigeria's colonial history was pre-dominantly written by British officials, none of whom would have it in their interests to criticise Empire in their accounts. Max Siollun (2021) deftly navigates the impact of colonisation on Nigeria in his excellent book, *What Britain Did to Nigeria*.

Maybe we should be asking young people 'for whom was the Empire a positive force?' After all, that appears to be a better question, because we can then start to unpick the idea of fairness, power and justice. In fact, the following are all better questions:

• In what ways was the British Empire built on violence?
• What are the lasting effects of Empire on colonised people?
• How can we hear the voices of the colonised in order to know what Empire meant to them?
• How does Empire affect society, culture and history in colonised countries?
• How are colonised people reclaiming their culture and society through decolonisation?

A tricky question that is almost always raised when thinking about how we teach Empire is on the idea of blame. Inevitably, someone will ask: but why should I be sorry for what people in the past have done? It's a good question, and possibly one that lies in our deep desire not to be criticised or to feel fallible.

There are some brilliant books that add to our understanding of how dominant narratives can be countered when it comes to Empire.

• *What Britain did to Nigeria* – Max Siollun
• *Empireland* – Sathnam Sanghera
• *Inglorious Empire* – Shashi Tharoor
• *The New Age of Empire: How Racism and Colonialism still Rule the World* – Kehinde Andrews

Counter-Narratives

• Provide multiple perspective on imperial activity.
• Openly discuss the language that might be used to describe Empire and its implications.
• Acknowledge the violence and oppression that took place in the British Empire.

Dominant Narrative: Race Determines Sporting Success

In 2001, a book appeared on the subject of the physical prowess of Black athletes that led to a flurry of documentaries and scientific articles. The book, entitled *Taboo: Why Black Athletes Dominate Sports and Why We're Afraid to Talk About It*, by Jon Entine (2001), posed theories that claimed to be based in science, suggesting that Black men have physical advantages over white men both in muscle composition and in the relative measurements of the torso. This view, in a society where Black men were excelling in sport, was basing their victories on genetics. Some have even claimed that you could find the root causes of this physical superiority in enslavement. The 'weak' enslaved people died out and those who survived were deemed physically fit as they had survived the ordeal.

Misconceptions appear in science and the teaching of Sports Science when we consider this dominant narrative. In fact, it is more true to say that when we omit the presence of this dominant narrative from the discourse, we leave young people to absorb inaccurate information from inaccurate sources.

This is where race as construct, not as biology, very much comes into play. In the teaching of these subjects, it must be made clear that social and cultural factors, not biology and genetics, play a bigger role in sporting success than anything else. Kerr (2010) points out the egregiousness of the claim that Kenyan athletes are biologically adapted to running long distances, alongside other examples of sporting fallacies.

There is also the issue of 'stereotype replication' in sports. Lola Adesioye (2008) commented in *The Guardian* that 'A 1999 study by the University of Arizona actually shows that so ingrained are the stereotypes about racial superiority and inferiority in certain sports that they affect not only which sports both black and white people gravitate toward but also their performance in those sports. What we see is what we are drawn to take part in.'

How does this show up in the PE curriculum and in other Sports Science subjects? Who do we laud as the exemplars of sporting success and what narratives do they perpetuate?

Counter-Narratives

- Present the field of research that shows that race is a social construct and distinct from biology.
- Ensure that there is visibility of counter-examples, especially in sports, that demonstrate the universality of sporting endeavour.
- Openly discuss misconceptions about race and sport – making sure that you are not inadvertently reinforcing false notions through exemplars.

Dominant Narrative: The East is Other

Edward Said, in 1978, published *Orientalism*, in which he defined three tenets of the term itself. Firstly, he posits that 'Anyone who teaches, writes about, or researches the

Orient – and this applies whether the person is an anthropologist, sociologist, historian, or philologist – either in its specific or its general aspects, is an Orientalist, and what he or she does is Orientalism.' He goes on to argue that Orientalism is also a systemic distinction between an exotic and troubling 'East' and a more acceptable 'west' when he states: 'Orientalism is a style of thought based upon an ontological and epistemological distinction made between "the Orient" and (most of the time) "the Occident".' He also notes in the third definition of the term that 'Orientalism can be discussed and analysed as the corporate institution for dealing with the Orient – dealing with it by making statements about it, authorizing views of it, describing it, by teaching it, settling it, ruling over it: in short, Orientalism is a Western style for dominating restructuring, and having authority over the Orient.' In other words, Orientalism is a system of control and superiority.

If you aren't aware of what Orientalism is, it is worth reading Edward Said's influential work on this topic. The concept of Orientalism is very much rooted in in a colonial and racist past and it is predicated on insidious beliefs about the people of the Middle East, North Africa, some parts of Central Asia and East Asia. Even in the terminology in describing the physical location of these vastly different peoples, we have learned over the years in our own schooling to describe East Asia as the 'Far East', denoting a mysterious, segregated and distant space in which the people are very much different from white Western Europeans.

My own reference points for the so-called Orient were defined by cultural reference points such as the *Carry On* films and T.E Lawrence epics, and *Indiana Jones and the Temple of Doom*. In these, the Orient is characterised as incomprehensibly different, comedic even, characterised by criminality and the occult, and steeped in racist ideas about eastern cultures.

Mariam Khalifa, in *Sail Magazine*, writes lucidly about the Orientalism of Aladdin. In the Disney film's original soundtrack, Agrabah is described as a land 'where they cut off your ear if they don't like your face, it's barbaric, but hey, it's home' (2016). Disney later rectifies this line as protestors quite rightly call it out as racist. Khalifa also points out the repeated declarations of Mulan's role as a girl – indicating time and time again that her status in her culture is inferior due to her gender. This is a recurring trope in Orientalism.

In fact, there are ways in which we can identify whether a piece of popular culture is engaged in Orientalism. In 'How to Spot Orientalism' Bridget Anscombe et al. provide a checklist that allows us to identify some of the problematic tropes of Orientalism.

Portrayal of Gender Stereotypes

- Does the environment seem patriarchal?
- Are Asian men being emasculated or presented as asexual?
- Do you see Lotus Blossom/Madame Butterfly/Dragon Lady characteristics in the female characters?

Cultural Representation

- Are aspects of Asian culture over-exaggerated for comedic relief?
- Are cultural objects unauthentically represented in the film?
- Are different Asian cultures represented as one?
- Are cultural practices overexaggerated in the film?

Yellow Face

- Are non-Asian actors pretending to be Asian or presenting Asian characteristics?
- Are actors exaggerating Asian accents for no specific reason?
- Are Asian actors representing other Asian cultures which they do not identify with ethnically in a degrading manner? (Anscombe et al., 2021)

Our role as teachers is to be able to identify potentially problematic presentations of the global locations identified in Said's theory, become aware of the impact of them in our curriculum, actively teach about these problematic portrayals and provide counter-material that allows for a better view of the people and places identified as the 'Orient'. It may be worth having a look at how this concept might come up in the curriculum.

In *Tales of Empire: Orientalism in Nineteenth-Century Children's Literature*, Brittany Renee Griffin (2012) outlines the connections between the global market as instigated by the East India Company and the anxiety of the imperial forces after the Indian Mutiny. Christina Rosetti's 'Goblin Market' is published a year after the Mutiny and portrays the exotic Goblin in contrast with the bucolic protagonists being lured by ripe exotic wares. The historical context of the text may need a reference to Orientalism and a definition of such.

Similarly, the concept of Orientalism may appear in readings of Sherlock Holmes. In *The Sign of Four* the reader is introduced to the racial characteristics of Tonga, the Andamanese character.

> It straightened itself into a little black man, the smallest I have ever seen with a great, misshapen head and a shock of tangled, dishevelled hair. Holmes had already drawn his revolver, and I whipped out mine at the sight of this savage, distorted creature. He was wrapped in some sort of dark ulster or blanket, which left only his face exposed, but that face was enough to give a man a sleepless night. Never have I seen features so deeply marked with all bestiality and cruelty. His small eyes glowed and burned with a sombre light, and his thick lips were writhed back from his teeth, which grinned and chattered at us with half animal fury. (Conan Doyle, 2009: 202–203)

This characterisation, combined with the exotic objects of Indian origin, and the association of India and Indians with criminality, needs direct address in the classroom. Contextual questions, or analysis of the language as related to context may illuminate the

Victorian consciousness of race and identity, and allow students to conduct a reading that examines attitudes towards 'the Other' in literature.

Counter-Narratives

- Provide examples of the East as a fully rounded entity.
- Acknowledge the power systems that have created the concept of the Orient.
- Show students examples of people and places with a non-Orientalist lens.

Dominant Narrative: Gay/Trans/Neurodivergent People are a Modern Phenomenon

One of my favourite dominant narratives is the belief that LGBTQ+ people are a modern phenomenon. I often joke that they must have arrived after the death of Queen Victoria, filing out of the closet in relief. I am minded to note all of the conversations that I have held about there not being any gay people in the past. How far back do we need to go to prove that sexuality has always been as varied as people themselves? Ancient China gives us the story of the leftover peach from the Spring and Autumn Era, in which male lovers share a peach. There is evidence in Ancient Hindu texts observing the presence of same-sex activities scientifically. Transgender people have existed for millennia, even if they were not called transgender as such. I could go on.

I have had similar conversations in which people have tried to convince me that there were no autistic people 'in the old days'. The history of autism as we currently understand it does stem from the 20th century, but it is early 20th-century study that identifies and diagnoses autism. There is speculation about historical figures who were reported to hold characteristics that may or may not signify autism, but it is very hard to say with any certainty.

The curriculum really does need to address these narratives, as they perpetuate a common belief and the implication that these identity groups are 'fashionable' or a trend amongst the youth of today. In this case, it is essential that we build in knowledge about identities and place them in the longest history possible for us to find. It counters the idea that we are in a 'phase'. It could appear in PSHE, in Child Development, in Sociology, as well as in assemblies and affinity group contexts.

Counter-Narratives

- Ensure that students understand the long histories of marginalised groups, moving beyond visibility in the 20th century.
- Meaningfully discuss how language has contributed to visibility for some marginalised groups.
- Explore the development of ideas on neurodivergence.
- Consider the vast amount of evidence that gender binaries are not fixed in many cultural contexts.

Dominant Narrative: Judaism can Only be Seen in Light of the Holocaust

How does a child encounter Judaism in the curriculum? It may well be that the religion itself is covered within the RE curriculum; however, statistics show that Judaism is one of the lesser studied religions according to the exam boards. In many schools where compulsory religious education is limited to three to four hours every fortnight, it is hard to provide any depth or nuance when educating students about Jewish history, culture, religious ritual and religious texts.

So how does a child develop their schematic understanding of a religion that has experienced a significant amount of hate, and has been subject to genocide? It may be the case that there is some representation of Judaism through characters in common literature in the UK. A child may experience a Jewish protagonist in the form of Shylock in *The Merchant of Venice*. A child may also experience a representation of Jewishness through the portrayal of Fagin in *Oliver Twist*. It is evident that both characters present problematic and indeed racist caricatures of Jewish figures, as evidenced by the stereotypical actions and appearances of both. It may be the case that these are the only representations of Jewish identity, or perceived Jewish identity, that children in secondary school in the UK ever experience. What are they to make of this information? The characters in question can only be couched in the realm of criminality and deviance.

The only other place where children encounter Jewish people is through the teaching of the Holocaust. Here we have the flipside of the coin: in this case the Jewish person is a passive victim, one whose broken body is testament to the evil of a regime in a particular space and time. This representation does not allow for any indications of agency as it is not often taught but there were significant rebellions against the Nazis from within the Jewish communities of the time. The counter-narrative to this may lie in the spotlighting of people who engaged in resistance.

One brilliant example is that of the *Kashariyot*: young Jewish women who engaged in resistance activities; another in the story of Rosa Heilman supporting resistance in Auschwitz. Or we could go further than the Holocaust and look at innovators such as Laszlo Biro, inventor of the ballpoint pen. Our students might know of Albert Einstein, but do they know he was Jewish, at least, as he deemed, culturally?

There are so many alternatives to be taught. A curriculum in which Jewish identity includes art, music, engineering and politics: it ought to be possible to teach a more three-dimensional view of Judaism and Jewish people, and yet, the three examples above seem to prevail within schools even in the 21st century.

Counter-Narratives

- Ensure that agency is considered when teaching about marginalised groups, especially in light of oppression and resistance.
- Openly discuss patterns of representation that skew narratives towards binaries such as passive victim/oppressor.

This chapter only covers some of the dominant narratives in existence and as they play out in the curriculum. I imagine we could collectively come up with even more dominant narratives that need unpicking with counter-narratives and I wish I could go into them all.

The key point here is to recognise thoughts and ideas that are generated by dominant narratives and to construct a curriculum that acknowledges how power structures have kept those dominant narratives in play, and then interrogates the counter-narratives that are possible.

REFLECTION QUESTIONS

- What are the dominant narratives in your subject?
- How can you interrogate the origins of these narratives?
- How can you provide counter-examples to support balancing out the narrative?

12

CASE STUDIES PART 1

HISTORY, SCIENCE AND MATHS

History

In this case study, Samir Richards explains the rationale and process of his work in diversifying the History curriculum

To give you some context, our school is in Luton, and is in one of the most deprived areas of an already deprived town. I want to touch on a few things which we do to ensure students in History make progress.

When my colleagues and I joined the school, the KS3 History curriculum was purely white European history. We changed this quickly after surveying parents and students for their views. Students mentioned they felt 'left out', that History 'was not for them'.

We proposed the changes we'd like to make and 98% (243 respondents) said the changes would be 'better' or 'much better'. We asked parents their thoughts – the overwhelming response (100%) is that they felt the changes would be 'positive' or 'significantly positive'. A lot has been discussed about whether a representative curriculum helps. Over 90% of our cohort at the school is British Pakistani/Bangladeshi. I believe these changes have been a key reason for our success this year.

Results were really poor from this school in History. When I joined the school, comments about how History is pointless from the students as they were not 'included' really struck me. One boy said History is an 'old white man's thing'. Another asked me why I and other colleagues of colour taught History when it's just boring white old men. One student from Caribbean descent spoke to me about how he felt embarrassed whenever slavery was taught and he believed it could and should have been taught better in schools. Additionally, I was 22 when I started this work – History curriculum in schools was fresh in my mind and I knew I was dissatisfied with it as a mixed heritage young person from Luton.

I knew that not including a diverse and representative curriculum is just bad history. It is for the same reason why you have people like Laurence Fox stating that including a turbaned soldier was for the 'woke mob'. In reality millions of Indians fought for the

British Empire and the fact one hasn't been included before or the fact it shocked many people to see this fact is more of a travesty than anything.

Behaviour was also poor in History. It was seen as a joke subject which many did not take seriously. We felt that students were unlikely to behave in a lesson if they feel excluded by the topic or how a topic is being taught. It was a reasonable assumption that academic performance would improve if the students felt involved in the lessons and History was for them.

I was struck by the statement in 'Thinking Beyond Boundaries' by Todd (2019: 6): 'The choices or emphases we make, in relation to the curriculum, are related to the exercise of power – perhaps unconsciously – in replicating our own histories, but with possible detrimental impacts for both the subject and those pupils who may see themselves excluded from this national story.' It made me realise how important it is to diversify the curriculum.

A couple of new colleagues arrived and we took on the task of turning the History department around and saw that results for the last couple of years were not great. We were working in a team of four with the previous Subject Team Leader at the time, too. That year we knew we needed to get improved 2019 results so our focus was on that, but we worked hard to map out where we wanted KS3 to look in the next few years.

There were lots of barriers, but time was a big one. One colleague was Head of Faculty and Assistant Head, I was an NQT, another a History teacher but then Head of House after Year 1. We all had other responsibilities and taught full timetables. This meant that any changes would have to be done in our own time. The changes were drastic and it took late nights for a number of years to do this work.

We made incremental changes every single year and even now we continue to update. One example was looking at misconceptions that are embedded from primary school and then perpetuated in secondary and via the internet: things like the use of the word 'slave' rather than 'enslaved person'; using the phrase 'potato famine' rather than what the Irish call it, 'The Great Hunger'. All of these are easy changes but embedded from an early age. Another barrier was dealing with the fact that not all teachers knew all of the new curriculum. This meant we had to work on ensuring misconceptions were not encouraged by them either. Medium-term plans with misconceptions outlined and how to avoid them were stated. Furthermore, a video from the teacher who had made the unit was created – this was filmed on Loom to talk about some golden nuggets around the unit.

One unit of work that was tremendously successful was 'Do sources show migration has enriched Luton?' This is a thematic local study. We go back all the way from the Romans to now and include groups like the Saxons, Normans, Triangular Enslaved Person Trade, Jewish, Caribbean and South Asian and its impact on Luton. Framing the question this way is definitely a leading question but counters some of the ideas students had picked up from the news/internet surrounding migration and its impact. In turn, it made them feel more positive about being in Britain and the contribution to our society from all migrants.

Before we came to the school (so 2018 results), at KS3, 10% of Year 7 students made no progress, and 32% of Pupil Premium (PP) students made no progress in comparison to 24% non-PP. I could see that those making 6+ sub-levels of progress were unevenly distributed to non-PP – 35% of students, in comparison only 29% PP students made this progress. Analysing the data I could see that progress in History was poor overall. KS4 2019 data were extremely poor and KS3 was worrying – we were setting up our KS3 students to have similar or even worse results than the 2019 GCSE results. The overall trend concerning the gap between PP and non-PP was troubling.

However, KS3 progress dramatically improved and importantly so did the PP data. In Year 7 only 2% of students made no progress in 2020–1; 66% of non-PP students made 6+ whereas 74% of PP students did. In Year 8 only 3% of students made no progress; 46% of non-PP students made 6+ levels of progress while 56% of PP students made 6+ levels of progress. What we witnessed was a huge shift at KS3. PP students were actually outperforming those who were not PP.

The Curriculum for Cohesion (Wilkinson, 2013) found the absence of an integrated History led to History education being seen as meaningless for many of these students and that History as a tool for civil success and knowledge is particularly important for Muslim boys. The Royal Historical Society in their *Race, Ethnicity and Equality in UK History* report contends that a lack of diversity in school and university curricula is partly responsible for the worryingly low number of BME students that take History at GCSE, A-level and degree level. The report further argues that this 'poses a genuine threat to our ability to maintain strong university History departments' (Royal Historical Society, 2018: 26). The disengagement of minority groups in Britain and their history education was further supported by a survey of students from minority ethnic backgrounds, concerning the History curriculum and its personal connection to them. It concluded that students felt a lack of connection to the largely white British history they learnt; they felt marginalised by what they perceived as narrowness of their curriculum and they did not share the sense of pride in Britain's achievements expressed by some white peers.

For anyone that knows me professionally they'd have heard me say 'you're good at things you enjoy and you enjoy what you're good at'. I think it applies to most things and what we saw is the boys now enjoying History. So we'd achieved 50% of the job by making these changes. There were some quick and easy changes that just made sense.

We also had conversations and Google forms at Open Evenings and Futures Evenings which we asked parents to complete. Before the changes parents commented that the History curriculum was not a reflection of the student body. The comments were as follows: 'this is the same as when I was in school' or 'this is what people learnt 20 years ago'.

We knew from this that the UK has changed since the parents were in school and 20 years ago. The curriculum should move with the times as the parents suggested. After the changes we also wanted to check parental views – parents were overwhelmingly positive. They were also pleased that Islam was being shown positively in the curriculum through the Golden Age scheme of work. They felt that Islam whenever usually mentioned outside of home or the private sphere of mosque, etc., it was when it was being criticised. They felt the topic would empower their sons to take pride in their identity and heritage. They commented that they noticed that negative portrayals in the media of Islam in Britain had an impact on mental health, belonging and identity.

A significant minority were also surprised by the World War I unit, 'Whose Voices Have Been Forgotten from the First World War?' To learn the impact of the Empire's soldiers and their experiences was a nice discovery for many who were not previously aware. However, many more commented that they *were* aware and they are glad that this is now being reflected in the curriculum – something they felt had previously been left out.

Students commented that they enjoyed learning about different areas of history. They especially liked the unit about the Mughals – the idea of a story and the narrative itself. They liked learning about the tolerance of the Royals centuries ago and the architecture which still exists today. And, of course, the battles too!

Finally, the Year 9s love the Israel–Palestine unit. Students felt that sometimes they were not allowed to speak about Israel–Palestine for fear of being told off. We wanted to ensure they learnt the narrative from both sides – using parallel histories to help us. This is so they can form their own opinions when presented with the views from both sides of the conflict. Again, this was greatly appreciated by students who could now hold intelligent, articulate conversations about the conflict rather than just arguing baselessly and without fact. In turn, it helped challenge their own preconceived ideas of how the conflict came about. Partition was a useful topic for all teachers as the British Empire and its impact in countries was quite well known but this area was not. Students appreciated learning this.

We also use good history – for the Empire unit we use Sathnam Sanghera's (2021) book *Empireland*, thus introducing students to authors and historians from a diverse background. Others used include David Olusoga, Shashi Tharoor, Miranda Kauffman and Stephen Bourne. We felt this was important because the Royal Historical Society said diversification of the curriculum must include revision both of the content and of the scholarship used to inform that content.

A quote that really stuck with me through these changes was from W.E.B. Du Bois:

> How easy, then, by emphasis and omission to make children believe that every great soul the world ever saw was a white man's soul; that every great thought the world ever knew was a white man's thought; that every great deed the world ever did was a white man's deed; that every great dream the world ever sang was a white man's dream.(Du Bois, 1920, cited in Verso Books, 2020)

Science

Emma Swift and Natalie Johnston, Trust-Wide Subject Leads for Science, outline how they considered diversity in Science

When you begin to think about the Science curriculum and how to better ensure that your curriculum embraces, celebrates, highlights and foregrounds diversity we found it helpful to review the current schemes of work and resources through different lenses. The lenses that we selected were taken from the Equality Act 2010 and are shown below.

- Sex
- Transgender
- Disability
- Race
- Sexuality

But I Just Have to Teach the Science...

The Science curriculum is generally more prescriptive in terms of content than most subjects, with most secondary schools following the National Curriculum in KS3 and a combined or separate science course at GCSE. We also know that the time to teach the course can be extremely tight, so we recommend that you ensure that this process is part of the usual cycle of curriculum review. A lot of this work is just about auditing what you have, looking at the sequencing and then swapping or adding things in. This is an iterative process and will develop over time. In many schools, diversity is a part of any curriculum review.

When reviewing your curriculum, you should seek opportunities to:

- Challenge dominant narratives by usualising and embedding diverse representation.
- Expand the domain of valued knowledge by including diverse curriculum linked knowledge, which is an act of subject knowledge enhancement.

We are aware that diverse voices are underrepresented in all levels of scientific endeavour and as educators need to be aware that without careful thought about a science scheme of work, we can inadvertently support this disparity. If we don't highlight diverse voices we lead to a distortion through omission.

Adding Context to the Narrative

Look at the representation within your curriculum. As Science teachers we have to talk about the scientists who have contributed to significant discoveries in science, and the recorded majority of these are white men. It is important to teach the stories of scientists who have changed our view of the universe; however, it is also important to take the opportunity to talk to students about the social and economic reasons why science was mainly investigated by men in the past. It is also important to highlight the occasions when women or global majority people have made contributions which were hidden or erased from the record. An unintended consequence of teaching the male-dominated Science curriculum is that it may leave students with the idea that global majority, female, LGBT and disabled people are:

- Not historically significant.
- Have no agency/power.
- Should only be studied in light of their relationships with men.
- Victims.

Paralleling Stories

So you can challenge this. You should take opportunities to parallel the contributions of underrepresented groups (global majority, female and disabled scientists) when you teach the traditional scientists and their individual contributions. Do you talk about Rosalind Franklin when talking about Crick and Watson? Or Jocelyn Bell Burnell's discovery of pulsars when looking at space discoveries in parallel with Galileo's discovery of the moons of Jupiter?

Consider when you can take the opportunity to highlight scientists whose contributions are not highlighted by the GCSE specification; however, beware of encounter hierarchy. Students tend to believe that the first piece of information that is shared with them is the most important. So, when you are talking about fission can you highlight the contributions of Lise Meitner, or Rachel Carson when speaking about bioaccumulation?

Different Examples – Representative Images

When you use images to represent situations are they of white, able-bodied men? If so, is there opportunity to swap these to show a more representative image of British society. This includes the opportunity to increase the challenge and challenge misconceptions when teaching topic like genetics. Would the use of an example with a mixed race (biracial) family when teaching genetics open the door for a more complex discussion about polygenic rather than single genetic manifestation of human variation?

The Vacuum Effect

We also know that often the only time students may encounter some of these phenomena and ideas is in their Science lessons, and therefore we need to be careful about the vacuum effect. This is where a curriculum fails to build a context around an idea which allow a bias to propagate. For example, when teaching about genetic disorders you may choose to study sickle cell anaemia, which in the UK is most commonly seen in people of African and Caribbean backgrounds. Including this topic in the curriculum allows visibility and representation. In addition, it is an excellent example to include as it allows you to link learning from natural selection, evolution, blood role and function to the recessive and dominant alleles in genetic disorders. This is because having a sickle cell trait provides malarial protection, but having sickle cell anaemia does not. However, if you taught this without context, you may lead to the misconception that different races are significantly different in their genetic makeup.

Different Examples - Challenging Stereotypes

Following on from the use of images you can look to highlight the contributions of people with protected characteristics in questions. When writing speed questions, for example, absolutely use Usain Bolt's 100 metre record breaking time, however, could you also include Jonnie Peacock's 2016 Paralympic win in Rio in the 100 metre T44 of 10.81 seconds? If using swimming as an example, could you use Ellie Simmonds' world record breaking swim at the Rio Paralympics, where Simmonds defended her gold medal for the 200 metre individual medley, setting a new world record – the first below 3 minutes at 2:59.81?

Obviously, these are only two examples but as you move through your curriculum you will see multiple examples to include disabled, female or global majority representation. Try also to avoid the only positive representations of BAME people being in sport.

Check Your Pronouns and Your Names

A simple way to see if your resources are diverse is to check your pronouns. Do you tend to use 'he' when talking about doctors and astronauts in questions? And how often as staff do we do the same thing when teaching? When writing questions, are the names representative of society as a whole or is there an imbalance in the gendering or the ethnicity?

There are lots of really great resources to challenge gender stereotyping in science from the Institute of Physics: www.iop.org/about/publications/improving-gender-balance

Problematic People

There are a number of people who we should teach about as they made significant contribution to science. However, some of these people had some problematic views on both race and gender. The majority of these scientists' views can be explained through the context of the time in which they lived (Darwin and Carl Linnaeus to name a few).

However, some of them, like James Watson, continue to make claims which are problematic and use science to support these views. It is important to address these ideas with the students and challenge them. Challenging Watson's views and views like these is part of my commitment to being anti-racist.

There are lots of great books about race, gender and science. Speak to the literacy coordinator: could they be included on any school reading lists?

- *How to Argue with a Racist: History, Science, Race and Reality* – Adam Rutherford
- *Inferior: The True Power of Women and the Science that Shows it* – Angela Saini
- *Superior: The Return of Race Science* – Angela Saini

Sensitivity Around Language

Look at the language you use particularly around sex and gender and empower teachers to feel confident in using correct terms. This comes up when teaching topics like chromosomes, which could be an opportunity to highlight the difference between biological sex and gender, which in turn might ensure that all students are included. Try to ensure that all staff (and students) use a common language when talking about things like people who are intersex. Ensure that all staff feel confident to talk about topics like intersex knowledgeably. A good website to help with these issues is Schools Out: www. schools-out.org.uk

Maths

Angel Hinkley talks us through some of her thoughts on diversity in Maths

Our young people are attempting to figure out who they are and where they fit in the world. As educators, we have a responsibility to equip them with the tools they need to feel they belong, rather than feel like an imposter. Every young person understands there is a bigger picture; they have a connection to the rest of the world, and a sense of being part of a global community. The Maths we practise and use today originates from across the world. If all young people understand this sense of community, why they are connected, racism can be reduced because many unconscious biases will be removed. Decolonisation of the curriculum is about developing our understanding of the bigger picture and reaching out beyond our own environment. It is another strategy for teaching Maths. It increases young people's mathematical knowledge. Decolonising the curriculum in Maths is adding people/events/ideas/learning strategies. The narrative of such events should be meaningfully connected to the learning. This will help to ensure that decolonising the curriculum does not fall into the trap of adding tokenistic stories, but to develop a deeper understanding of world history as a series of interconnected events. Lessons are inspiring all young people to open their mind to the wider world they might not yet know.

We took part in a three-step process that involved:

- Emphasising career-long professional learning.
- Creating resources.
- Sharing with others.

Here are some examples of the results of our thinking:

Example 1

Frequently asked questions in Maths are 'What is the point of this?' and 'When would I ever use this?' In Egypt, around 2500 BCE the Pyramids of Giza were built. Pythagoras' theorem, which enables you to make a right-angle triangle, was one of the techniques employed. Maths has been used to help create one of the Seven Wonders of the World, that has stood for over 4000 years. By using this example, the concept of Maths becomes much more relevant and useful.

When I teach Pythagoras, I use a map or globe to show where in the world this historic event occurred. We then move northeast to Iraq, Iran and Syria, where I explain that there is archaeological evidence of the Babylonians learning Pythagoras' theorem in schools around 2000 BCE.

The young people are taken aback by the knowledge that schools even existed all those years ago. I always ask them why this evidence has come as such a surprise to them. 'They couldn't have had lessons all those years ago', 'They wouldn't have been that advanced back then'. Another interesting fact is that Pythagoras was born approximately 570 BCE, many years after the pyramids were built and Babylonian pupils learned his theorem; this could be because as a young adult, he had travelled to Egypt and Babylon. This leads to more discussions in class, and it's a topic that mathematicians and historians are still debating today.

The impact is clear. Throughout this topic young people are exploring the origins of mathematics; they are immersed in historical evidence of human populations; they are guided in their conceptual understandings. They are making connections in learning by reaching beyond traditional norms. All of this is achieved in a way where the facts are not presented as abstracted or disconnected.

Example 2

At our school, the young people are introduced to the abacus with an explanation of who and where it was created and how to use it. Young people also enjoy the sensory experience that the abacus provides.

Below is a conversation I had with one of the young people.

Young person: Ms Hinkley, abacuses were invented by the Chinese.

AH: Yes.

Young person: I love the Chinese because they have made Maths easy for me.

She then went on to explain why the abacus helps her with her Maths.

Impact

The young person has a positive understanding of how we are global citizens and how other countries are helping her with her Mathematics.

Example 3

On marking a young person's work, the answer given was $10 + 6 = 7$. On asking how she came to that number I realised she had calculated the sum $1 + 6 = 7$. She thought the zero was worth nothing, she didn't understand its place value.

This is an intelligent young person who is very well read and always has a book on her desk. She loves to read. She has a barrier with Maths. She was taught the place value system in the past, so I focused my teaching on her strength, storytelling.

'We're going to India, where an Indian mathematician invented the number zero', I said, picking up the globe. 'This was an amazing invention because the number zero has the ability to change the value of a number. For example, 7 with a zero in front becomes 70, and 7 with two zeros in front becomes 700.'

Looking at the original question, the young person replied, 'That is not 7, that is 16.'

Impact

When the mathematical concept was explained in a way that the young person could grasp, she found where her mistake was through understanding. She was given an example that linked the maths she was learning in class to another part of the world. Her learning had a meaningful connection.

The potential for enhanced learning is huge. It adds connections and relevance by placing learning on a global stage. This is an active and creative process. For me to decolonise the curriculum at a high school in Glasgow, I realised that the first step was to explain why it is crucial for our school to embark on a journey of racial literacy development and understand the value of being an active anti-racist school instead of a non-racist school. We need to go beyond our own walls to add relevance, access and opportunity for all.

13
CASE STUDIES PART 2
GEOGRAPHY, LANGUAGES AND MUSIC

Geography

Jodie Powers, Assistant Headteacher, has undertaken work in Geography to diversify the curriculum

One of the core concepts that underpins Geography is place. When planning a Geography curriculum, it is important to carefully consider the places you will explore and the stories about each place that you will tell. A key starting point for me when considering the narratives about places is Chimamanda Ngozi Adichie's TED Talk on *The Danger of a Single Story*. The message is clear: be careful about the way you present people and places as that can become the defining story of those people and places. Therefore, it is important to consider how places are presented within a curriculum and whether places are being represented in a single dimension:

- Africa is a continent full of poor people.
- Haiti was affected by a bad earthquake in 2010.
- China is a country only known for the One-Child Policy.
- Squatter settlements all lack access to basic services.

Or are you developing pupils' understanding of a place, as well as utilising it as a geographical case study?

The study of place underpins our curriculum from Year 7 through to Year 11. Often places are used to explore the core geographical content we want pupils to learn. For example, utilising development indicators to assess the level of development within a country or exploring a river's course from source to mouth. The curriculum that has been constructed is one that has a spiral narrative. Consequently, pupils can revisit the core geographical content, in increasing complexity as they progress through Key Stage 3.

One topic that enables pupils to develop their geographical knowledge is the Year 8 topic of Africa and Kenya. These two topics allow pupils to utilise and expand their knowledge of climate, biomes and development indicators that were introduced to pupils in Year 7, as well as developing further knowledge about natural resources, tectonic hazards and types of industry.

Within the KS3 National Curriculum Africa is mentioned twice:

- Locational knowledge: using maps of the world to focus on Africa – on its environmental regions, key physical and human characteristics, countries and major cities.
- Place knowledge: understanding geographical similarities and differences and links between places through the study of human and physical geography of a region within Africa.

Africa is the world's second largest continent, containing 54 countries, and leading to a vast array of potential themes to explore. Thus, one of the first starting points was to develop the purpose and aims of the topic, utilising the National Curriculum as guidance:

- Challenging pupils' misconceptions about the continent.
- Identifying the key physical characteristics to be covered: biomes, rivers, Rift Valley.
- Identifying the elements of human geography to be covered. Naturally the continent lends itself to covering elements of development: the contrast between rich and poor and the growing inequality between and within countries in Africa as well as exploring the reasons for these differences.

Once the core ideas had been identified, the research began. A wide range of books were used to deepen my own understanding of the continent and the human elements of geography that were to be covered in this topic:

- *Africa is Not a Country* – Dipo Faloyin
- *The Looting Machine* – Tom Burgis
- *The Divide: A Brief Guide to Global Inequality and its solutions* – Jason Hickel

There were also several articles written in *Teaching Geography*, and further internet research that was carried out to create a secure and up-to-date evidence base for the lesson content.

Within the new Scheme of Learning, pupils' misconceptions about Africa are 'busted' within the first lesson, including the common one in geography that 'Africa is a country'. Within this lesson, pupils analyse and disprove Band Aid's lyrics in 'Do They Know it's Christmas' as well as reading excerpts from Tim Marshall's *Prisoners of Geography* and Dipo Faloyin's *Africa is Not a Country*. Both extracts serve to provide a context for the

Table 13.1   Adapting the Geography curriculum

Old Scheme of Learning Africa & Kenya	New Scheme of Learning What misconceptions do we have about Africa?
1. Africa or not?	1. Africa is not a country.
2. Life in Kenya.	2. What are the human and physical features of Africa?
3. Rural Kenya.	3. What opportunities are there on the continent of Africa?
4. Urban Kenya.	4. What challenges does the continent of Africa face?
5. Assessment: a migrant's diary.	5. How can Africa's challenges be managed?
6. Where do people in Kenya live?	*Please note once pupils have completed the above sequence of learning, they study the country of Kenya in greater depth.*
7. Tourism in Kenya.	

subsequent lessons looking at the opportunities and challenges that Africa's geography has created.

Pupils then navigate through a sequence of lessons looking at Africa's natural resources, the opportunities this provides but also the challenges, using ideas from Burgis's *The Looting Machine* and the idea of being 'resource cursed'. Pupils also explore some of the strategies to manage Africa's challenges including aid and fairtrade, culminating in pupils examining the sustainability of both strategies.

A key challenge was to ensure that the subject knowledge of colleagues was up to date so that the curriculum could be delivered as intended. Using department CPD time, colleagues were issued with subject knowledge audits, allowing them to identify their strengths and areas for development. Colleagues then identified an area of subject knowledge that they felt needed further development and began researching their chosen topic, using subject association memberships. After half a term of research a subject symposium was held where colleagues shared their research findings and the impact it had had on their teaching. Powerful discussions have arisen not only over subject knowledge but also pedagogical approaches about how best to deliver the curriculum.

Perhaps one of the greatest challenges in Geography is that the world is constantly evolving and so when studying human geography, in particular, the study of places within the curriculum must be reviewed to ensure that the content that is being taught to pupils is up to date. The same principle also applies to developing the subject knowledge of colleagues, and so ensuring that there are links to current articles or suggestions of wider reading within the schemes of learning is also an important element of ensuring the curriculum is delivered in the manner it was intended.

Finally, an important next step is to gather the opinions of pupils. Whilst staff regularly reflect on the topics and lessons taught across the curriculum, pupil voice is an area that we are yet to explore in depth. As such, facilitating conversations with pupils to ascertain the elements of the curriculum they value and those that they value less is important in ensuring that the desired intent of the curriculum is being communicated effectively to pupils through the lessons they study.

Languages

Luke Moffat, Head of Faculty for Languages, explains his approach to diversifying the curriculum

Modern Foreign Languages should liberate students from insularity and open their eyes to the outside world. This is even more relevant for schools in certain contexts, where students struggle to see that the world is a bigger place than the microcosm in which they exist. This describes our context and is similar to that of many schools across the country. We are the only secondary school in a medium-sized town, which is part of the largely rural county of Worcestershire. Whilst slowly changing, our student body isn't made up of many ethnicities and is not, traditionally, very diverse. If you are different from the usual white, heterosexual, 'British' stereotype, the chances are you will stand out. It is also worth mentioning here that many of our students struggle with low aspirations, not atypical of many schools with a similar context. This was very similar to my own school experience, in the same county, although my school days were affected by the lasting effects of Section 28, given that I started secondary school in 2003, just before it was repealed.

The change in our curriculum was, at first, gradual. It began with a really thought-provoking conversation with my line manager about the way in which we teach MFL. Before that conversation, everything I knew about MFL teaching was from the pedagogical principles that I had been taught whilst doing teacher training and through the input of more experienced colleagues during the early part of my teaching career: introduce single words, do various activities to consolidate, build up to a sentence level, more consolidation and then advance to the next unit of work. I am not criticising this approach per se, but there was a niggle at the back of my mind – was this ambitious enough for our young people? At the time, I was doing lots of research on the curriculum from various experts within our profession. Mary Myatt's work really resonated with me and then I stumbled upon a piece of work from Myatt & Co focusing on the power of story and narrative within our curriculum. This was the first brush stroke on my blank canvas of diversity.

Initially, we started with a trial for only one year group who were studying Spanish, due to staffing at that time. We created three characters that we wanted our students to invest in. I named one 'Abbud Rashīd' – this was important to me as Spain has a prominent Muslim community. The decision initially met with some resistance from colleagues. Accounts of having to remove Islam from the KS3 Religious Education curriculum due to a number of parental complaints and Islamophobia were given as cautionary tales. To me, this was exactly the reason to persist. We are here to educate: MFL is the perfect vehicle to open minds and hearts to the world outside of a student's insular bubble.

I still vividly remember April 2022 as a major turning point for me both professionally and personally. The Netflix blockbuster *Heartstopper* (based on the graphic novel of the same name) was on the cusp of being released; the hype was incredible. Little did I know that this show would propel me into being extremely passionate about queer representation within school. Soon afterwards, I produced resources for Pride Month, LGBT Month, restarted our PRIDE Club and led our whole-school Diversity Week. I wanted my faculty area, MFL, to be the most inclusive part of the school – every student would feel welcome. Our curriculum would transform from a heteronormative paradise to one where differences were celebrated. Students would feel empowered to be themselves, whoever that might be. We went from a curriculum based on single words to one that was led by an openly gay character, a bisexual secondary character, a Muslim character with African roots and many more. Students were finally seeing the whole world and not just their small world. Similarly, the faculty has evolved – we have become an MFL faculty that truly looks outward – in fact, it has become a key part of our staff recruitment process. Inclusivity is not a bolt on and it is important that potential additions to our faculty share our ethos. A recent survey conducted by Just Like Us, revealed that only 15% of teachers are comfortable discussing LGBT topics with students; the same percentage as three years ago. I am certain that since my appointment as Head of Faculty in 2021, this wouldn't be the case for our faculty.

I am proud of many things. The work that myself and my team have invested in over the last year and a half has been fundamental to me accepting myself. As I reflect on the possible barriers that could have existed, I understand how fortunate I am to have encountered barely any. My SLT (senior leadership team) line manager has been supportive, my team has embraced the vision with gusto, supporting me every step of the way, and students have been overwhelmingly positive about the characters and style of our lessons. In terms of social media, we have been so grateful for the positive reactions and feedback from colleagues around the country. Our posts about diversity and inclusion are amongst our most popular. We still do get negativity on social media. On a post regarding our LGBT MFL Library for example, we had approximately 100 comments – two of which were negative, with one stating that they are glad their child doesn't go to our school.

Diversity and inclusivity permeate every aspect of what we do, including our Schemes of Work. All of our classrooms have LGBT Pride flags, posters to educate students on diversity and signs to demonstrate that everyone, irrespective of any difference, is welcome. This being said, there are many concrete examples of how our schemes of learning have changed but some noticeable highlights include the way in which our students are introduced to colours in a foreign language. Our characters are the vehicle through which we deliver language content to our students and Marceau, our main character, is immensely proud of his LGBT identity and consequently uses a range of Pride flags to impart the key knowledge of colours. Not only does this demonstrate inclusivity, but it also allows us to promote diversity and encourage discussion about different LGBT identities. By dealing head-on with vocabulary such as gay, lesbian and bisexual we can help reduce prejudice and misinformation which might otherwise exist among Year 7 students. We can explain exactly what these terms mean and empower students who are questioning their identity to feel that they can do this safely. This contrasts markedly with our previous lesson, in which we taught colours using a variety of animals.

Other examples include the use of LGBT literature from France and Spain used in diversity week with KS4 and 5. For example, we used Adam Silvera's *They Both Die at the End* in French and *History is All That You Left Me* in Spanish. For KS3, we are planning how we can use more LGBT literature in lessons – especially literature originally written in the Target Language (rather than translated). Also, when teaching daily routine we build in discussion of the prayers that are an essential part of the daily routine for Muslims.

Although it is too early to see any hard evidence of the impact of this new approach to our KS3 curriculum in terms of outcomes, we have lots of anecdotal evidence of how it is making a difference to our students. For example we have Year 7s who are empowered to write down that they are proud to be lesbian or bisexual. Where else do they get this opportunity in most schools? KS3 students, inspired by our curriculum, make up a significant part of the PRIDE Club I relaunched last year, clearly feeling safe to be themselves. Our long-term goal is to have a diversity student leadership group who will help to transform our school curriculum. MFL have been the trail-blazers but other faculties should also be encouraged to become as inclusive and diverse as possible. Finally, I would like to end with a quote from a recent questionnaire I carried out with the PRIDE Club. A Year 8 student stated: 'I love going to French lessons because I feel safe and seen – this doesn't happen in other lessons.' This truly epitomises the need to embrace diversity and put inclusivity at the centre of everything we do!

Music

Gemma Sheppard walks us through her diverse curriculum

Curriculum development is continuous in all subjects. Due to its ever-changing nature, Music is expected to be current as well as include historical eras and global traditions. That's a pretty big ask, made an even bigger challenge by issues faced in many schools such as limited timetabling, facilities and specialist staff. Nevertheless, it is crucial that we also make progress in diversifying and decolonising the Music curriculum. Being able to plan most of our curriculum gives us the privileged opportunity to address misconceptions, marginalisation, white-washing, and improve representation of the young people we teach. With this in mind, we have begun to make conscious changes when evaluating our curriculum each year at our school; although it is important to note that this work is ongoing, not complete. I would like to share a number of adaptations that we have made to diversify our curriculum and the students' experiences so far.

We believe that the truly successful promotion of learning to play an instrument is dependent on all pupils being represented and included. We are lucky to be able to run a sub-curriculum alongside our main Year 7 lessons which gives students the opportunity to learn an instrument for free in groups of 15. The students receive an hour of instrumental tuition each week and the whole year group is covered a term at a time thus removing any cultural or financial barriers to getting involved. This has helped normalise being a musician at Langley. The curriculum has been written in-house and we selected the trombone (using very cost effective pBones) and violin (hired from our local Music hub) in order to challenge gender stereotypes. We had the teaching hours available in our staffing, so no extra cost was involved in that respect.

During the Year 7 main Music curriculum for Spring, students follow a typical Western orchestral instruments scheme of learning, but we have ensured that videos and pictures used are ethnically diverse. Some examples we use are the Chineke Youth Orchestra audition for *Britain's Got Talent*, New York's Harmony Program string family demonstrations and 'George Meets the Orchestra' by the Sydney Youth Orchestra Philharmonic. The scheme of learning concludes with a focus on keyboard instruments and skills, using clips of Isata Kanneh-Mason and blind, neurodivergent pianist Lucy from Channel 4's series *The Piano*. They are both breath-takingly inspirational in demonstrating where dedication can take you.

In our Year 7 Summer term curriculum, we have worked on the use of language and breadth of styles covered. The scheme of learning, entitled 'Crossing Continents', covers several music traditions originating from across the globe. We have replaced the phrase 'world music' to prevent students with similar traditions or experiences outside of school from feeling separated. We have also addressed conflation by identifying Ghanaian Drumming by its specific country instead of generalising as African Drumming. The second half of the term is a celebration of fusion and new styles created because of cultures coming together. This includes cross-curricular Salsa dancing, learning to play features of Bhangra and the year is rounded off with a Samba band performance.

Other examples of inclusive representation, wider breadth of styles and more considered use of language are included in Years 8 and 9. In Year 8's Summer term lessons, we use performances by the 100 Voices of Gospel to identify key stylistic features and conclude the year studying music traditions from a small number of named Caribbean islands, including Merengue from Dominican Republic, Trinidadian Calypso (with a mini unit on Ukulele), and an analysis of three of Bob Marley's biggest hits. The final scheme of learning in Year 9 begins with the development of musicals in which we use a video performance of 'Schuyler Sisters' from *Hamilton* for a comparison listening task and discuss why Porgy and Bess was so progressive. For lyric writing inspiration and improved understanding of verse–chorus structure, we use a variety of example singer song-writers including Khalid and Stevie Wonder.

A third focus in curriculum writing has been to include alternative Classical listening repertoire, moving away from pieces only written by white male composers. An example is the replacement of a Mozart symphony listening task with one that analyses the opening of Florence Price's *Symphony No. 1*. To avoid being tokenistic, Price's background as the first African American woman to be recognised as a symphonic composer is also discussed, including how she gained a place at the New England Conservatory of Music as it was one of the few places to accept African American students. Despite that, she was still thought to have had to claim to be Mexican to avoid racial discrimination. It is a happy coincidence that this lesson falls within Black History Month, although this is not the only time we want to give students the opportunity to talk about composers and artists that have been erased or neglected in the history books.

In Year 9, we have also diversified the film music examples we use as previously the unit was based entirely on the work of John Williams and Monty Norman. Now, the soundtrack from Disney's *Soul* and Quincy Jones's 'Soul Bossa Nova' also feature, as well as music from the *Black Panther* series, which has more diverse representation in its main characters. The Spring term in Year 8 covers Mozart's *Twelve Variations on Ah, vous dirai-je, maman*, Beethoven's *Symphony No. 5* and Holst's *The Planets Suite* as well as their stories, but there are opportunities to make links to other styles here too. An example is using *Musical Contexts* Ground Bass task that compares Pachelbel's *Canon in D* to Coolio's track *C U When U Get There* that samples its bass line.

The final aspect we have worked on is our delivery of the history of the Blues to make it clearer that early Blues music shares the experiences of musicians that were slaves and that the style developed after slavery was abolished. This coincides with our History Department's scheme on the same topic and gives students the opportunity to write their own lyrics empathetically about how people would have felt having their freedom taken away. Following an excellent Music Mark webinar by Syreeta Neal, curated by music educator Nate Holder, we have also updated the scheme to include current artists, for example *Bloodlines* by Kenny Neal.

There is definitely still much work to do regarding questioning sources and including more detailed background stories of the styles and artists we have chosen for our curriculum, but we're making progress and find that making time for professional development such as webinars, research and discussions within teams is crucial to instigating and supporting this important change.

14

FREQUENTLY ASKED QUESTIONS

If I do not have any of the protected characteristics, can I legitimately support this DEI work?

You do not need to 'qualify' to do DEI work. If you are passionate about the need for social change, and you believe in supporting those with protected characteristics, then that is a brilliant starting point. You might find that you need to spend some time in the learning zone – that beautifully scary space where you might feel uncomfortable with the things you are learning and realising. This is exactly the process we all go through when we are 'unlearning' our perceptions, our realms of understanding and our inherited ideas. This question is posed so often in training sessions I have run, and it often starts with: 'I am just a straight, white woman/man…'. You are not 'just' anything. Your allyship is central to success.

There are some ideas that you might want mull over when thinking about your role in DEI work if you do not have the protected characteristics you are advocating for. If your work if centred around you – your role, your feelings, the impact on injustice on you – then perhaps your focus needs to shift so that the protected characteristic is centred, and you are amplifying others' voices to ensure that there is integrity to the work.

To check this, consider where your ideas and influences come from. Are they solely manifestations of your own beliefs, or are you reading widely around the people and ideas you wish to provide allyship for? There is a body of work around identity that can be tapped into, interrogated and referred to regularly in your allyship.

I work in a monocultural school, do I need a diverse curriculum?

If you work in a context where the staff and student body is largely homogeneous, there is even more of a need to shape a curriculum in which diversity is embedded. Knowledge about difference – and the inherent value of difference – should not be left to chance. After all, where will your students get their impressions of people with disabilities, or LGBTQ+ folks if they are not getting a crafted and curated version of the world from you, the expert in the room? Remember the endgame on this one. Sending students into the world unprepared to value different cultures and identities in a meaningful way is a job poorly done.

Here I would refer back to the Professor Rudine Sims Bishop metaphor of 'mirrors, windows and sliding glass doors' (Bishop, 1990: ix–xi). A diverse curriculum allows students to not just see themselves but to see outside of themselves.

I feel my leadership team is not supportive of a diverse curriculum – what do I do?

Sometimes you have to find your own wind to blow a ship in a certain direction. If you feel that this work is not valued by your leadership team, as Brené Brown says: 'clear is kind'. And you have a choice to stay and try and change everyone around you, or whether to take you and your values elsewhere, where there is more alignment.

I have to teach X text – how do I approach it?

This question often pops up in relation to teaching of texts that include racial slurs, or problematic depictions of identities. I think of it as the *Of Mice and Men* question. For those of you who have never had the pleasure of teaching this text ad nauseum for the last 20 years, let me summarise. John Steinbeck writes about two migrant workers (including one with a learning disability) in Great Depression California, travelling to a ranch, meeting a Black man called Crooks, a man with a disability called Candy, and a 'seductive' and lonely woman named for her status as her husband's possession – Curley's Wife. The plot ensues. No spoilers, but it doesn't end well for anyone.

The book is as beautiful as it is problematic, not least because it holds a revered place in English curricula. It is worth interrogating why – is it because it is the seminal early 20th-century text about power? Or is it because it made its way into the exam syllabus and even when it was unceremoniously dumped during the Gove years from the exam specifications, it wheedled its way into the Key Stage 3 curriculum?

The problem lies in the fact that, despite the novella's focus on the hierarchies of power and personal look at inequality in society, all of the marginalised and vulnerable characters lose in some way. And of course, it includes numerous references to the 'n' work in reference to the sole Black character. Some teachers are highly uncomfortable reading the word aloud and refuse to do so, some talk to students beforehand to warn them that it will be read aloud. Maybe just choose another text.

My local community is not comfortable with us teaching about LGBTQ+ content, how do I approach this?

It is tricky to balance the needs and wants of our communities when creating the curriculum and there can be disagreement about what should be taught and what should not. In essence, schools have a responsibility to ensure that students have access to information about different relationships, including same-sex relationships, through

RSE in the primary phase (made mandatory in 2020), and in secondary, there is a responsibility to teach about sexual orientation and gender identity as part of RSE. It is important to acknowledge faith perspectives on sexuality and the legalities of opting out during various phases.

What about GCSE – its narrow focus means that we do not have the time or space, or necessity to diversify the curriculum.

It is true to say that GCSE specifications do have a more narrow focus than that of Key Stages 1, 2, 3 or 5. Firstly, I'd question what the purpose of our teaching is; is it just to create pass grades at GCSE or is it to create scholars in our subjects so that they are compelled to go on to further study in our subject areas? Perhaps that is too simplistic. It occurs to me that Key Stage 4 is a mere two years, compared to the many that go before it and after it.

There are diverse options appearing at GCSE – choosing them is often seen as a brave step when we consider the time and resources needed to start teaching new content. Exam boards are providing support materials now to alleviate this burden.

We do not have time to change everything, so can we put all of this into one unit?

The key to this question is in recognising that not everything has to be taught in whole units. It would be unfair and unfeasible to suggest that diverse content has to exist in every single lesson. It is more important to think about the conscious crafting of the curriculum so that you have a usualised approach to diversity across subjects. It is worth considering how you can use the different structures in your curriculum for different purposes. Whole unit structures might be useful in History, or Art, or Music. Lesson sequences or single lessons might work better for other content. Finally, there is nothing wrong with constructing moments in your lessons that serve as a 'Did you know' curiosity-inducing story, or fact.

The art of curriculum design lies in decision making. Where we place our brush at any given moment means that we are making choices. To continue the heavy-handed metaphor, we can choose one colour or several combined. We can change a brush stroke, we can add detail, or take it away. As an artist makes decisions about the composition of a canvas, we do too as teachers choosing how to 'paint' the world and our society.

What about making our students feel British?

I do wonder whether we have a working definition of what it means to be British, over and above the tenets laid out in the 'British Values' document. In the absence of any clear definition (assuming it isn't cricket, tea and sarcasm), I propose the following. Britishness has been influenced and shaped by world culture; it has assimilated the presence of the new and the old, it exists, as many islands do, in the meeting of the seas that bring with them ideas and identities.

Britishness has always been global, and not parochial, either through Empire, or through the spread of the language through technology. It assumes an awareness of its past and how it has developed today's society standing on the shoulders of giants from all over the world.

If that is too high-falutin, then perhaps we ought to focus instead on what we want for our young people. A sharp eye on the past and present and future, an acute awareness of how people shape places. An understanding that you can be proud of your British heritage and be aware of its missteps and flaws.

I don't feel I have the knowledge to be able to diversify the curriculum. In short I don't even know what I don't know. How do I extend my subject knowledge?

I have some good news. In reading this book, you have started on a journey towards developing your understanding of the kinds of knowledge that you might want to include in your curriculum. The next steps are very much about how you approach your own subject knowledge development. What do you do daily, weekly, monthly, termly, to ensure that you have a detailed understanding of what you are teaching?

You might want to go back through this book and look at the many book recommendations I have made. I have tried to weave in as many as possible.

For anyone embarking on a journey to create curriculum content, there is a responsibility to stay abreast of the nuances of what we teach, how it is situated and how it is understood today.

15

CONCLUSION AND COMMITMENT TO ACTION

I loved school. I loved learning. It was my escape from reality. Nine-year-old me was immersed in what was put in front of me. I trusted my educators to tell me about the past, the present and the future. I believed they would tell me all that they could. But they didn't. Not maliciously, I don't think, but as a result of all that I have laid out here. The result was a child that grew into a woman feeling like there were pieces missing in her. I may have grown to be successful in my career. I had my qualifications, but I'm not sure I had a sense of myself.

In trauma theories, there is often a metaphor of what happens when fundamental aspects of care are missing from a young person's experience. It's like bricks missing at the foundation of a wall. That's what it feels like to miss education that tells you who you are, where you fit, how you and people like you have made the world. The wall might stand, but it is not stable and solid and neither does it have integrity. Why have I spent so long learning the 'bricks' that were missed in my education? Because I, and other people like me, need to be seen in the world and to see the world. That's how we know we are valued.

In many ways, this book does not contain all the answers in how to create a diverse curriculum. It does explore the many, complex questions that arise when we are deciding on and crafting content that will form the basis of a young person's understanding of the world.

It is clear that including diversity in the curriculum cannot be an act that takes place once, and then is never looked at again. Curriculum is never done. It is a marvellous beast based on shifting sands; our job is to tame it as best we can in the moment and then reflect on what it might need next, according to the landscape it sits in.

It occurs to me that curriculum design that is diverse and decolonised requires a series of commitments:

1   A commitment to unlearning our own education paradigms.
2   A commitment to recognising epistemic injustice.

3   A commitment to reshaping our understanding of knowledge.
4   A commitment to building new knowledge based on a de-centring of power
    systems.
5   A commitment to knowing about curriculum effectiveness.
6   A commitment to purposeful evaluation.
7   A commitment to hearing feedback and acting on it.
8   A commitment to watching the social landscape to ensure the curriculum stays fresh.
9   A commitment to developing our own subject knowledge outside of the
    established parameters.
10 A commitment to building a better understanding of the world.

The Ten Commitments, perhaps.

All of the steps you could undertake – from learning the theory behind a diverse curriculum, to going through the evaluation and adaptation process – require you to go
slowly. Gobekli Tepe was not built in a day.

So there are some remaining questions that you might want to answer now that
you've finished this book:

- What's next?
- Who do you need to talk to?
- How does your identity sit in this process?
- Where will you go to learn?
- How will you take people with you?
- When will you start to make changes?
- How will you know they have worked?

I am sure that I will be hearing from you about the work you are doing – and I can't wait.
If you do use social media, you might want to use a hashtag to collate the work being
done by educators all over the world to ensure that the curriculum is fit for purpose.
Can I suggest:

#MyDiverseCurriculum

It's not catchy or groundbreaking, but we can share our ideas, we can pool resources and
we can celebrate successes together. I know you'll inspire me with your work.

Most of all, I am looking forward to your students' responses. We know that given
half a chance, young people will step up, make their feelings known and move towards
action in the blink of an eye. You can see this in the quotations from students in
Pearson's (2020) *Diversity and Inclusion in Schools Report*:

> I'm passionate that there should be more diversity in the curriculum. So I
> wrote to my principal about this and I am now working with teachers and
> peers to explore and agree what topics we should be learning about, from
> Windrush to African Kingdoms. (Diego Bartolomeu, age 13)

On X (formerly known as Twitter), I asked whether students had given any feedback on being shown a diverse curriculum. The responses are enough for me to know that we are doing something right.

> I never thought I'd study a book that was so closely linked to me. (via Donal Hale, on introducing *Purple Hibiscus* into the curriculum)

> Partition history is important to be taught because it helps us understand how we got to be where we are now as a country or as a world. (via Ashmi Morjaria, from Year 6 students)

> We do a little unit on Patience Agbabi's version of *The Knight's Tale* at the end of term with Yr7, and in my lesson as we watched a video of her reading the prologue, as soon as I put the video on the board, a boy in my class said: 'oh my GOODNESS! She is black like me!' And when I told him she was Nigerian he absolutely lost his mind. It was so lovely. (via Neve Eyles)

> We have been studying Baghdad as part of global history; as Peter Frankopan said 'History should be about broadening horizons.' I think that history as both a subject and as a living growing thing is the same as a window that only those with unbiased minds can truly see clearly through. Global history is vital for us to have knowledge of because as humans we have the right to understand and be empowered by our knowledge. Therefore I believe we need to learn about global history to truly understand ourselves and the world we reside in.

> In addition, Peter Frankopan states that if we don't look at the whole jigsaw, instead of one piece of the puzzle in our 'back yard' then history will become boring and regarded as fanciful stories instead of the impactful role models we admire and aspire to be. (via Katie Amery)

Out of the mouths of babes.

Final Words

I didn't write this book to criticise all the work that has gone into making your curriculum. I set out to explore the ways in which the curriculum can be made beautiful, truthful and engaging for all students. But a book won't do that; only teachers can do that. I am immensely aware of the time, effort and knowledge that goes into creating learning sequences – I have been there.

I have been through a process of Unlearning. I like to think of the last few years as an exercise in examining what I thought I knew about the world, education and curriculum building and unpacking it slowly, so that I made room for new knowledge, knowledge that I had missed, knowledge that had been pushed to the margins. It has taken time, and I am not finished, because, in all honesty, I don't think we can ever be finished in learning and unlearning and re-learning.

This is what I hope for you and your students. That you will find delight in curiosity; that you will revel in the lost stories; that you will feel indignation at the power imbalances that have defined curriculum in the past and still do today; that you will see yourselves; that you will learn how to exist with validation.

I'll leave you with Nelson Mandela and your thoughts.

Education is the most powerful tool which you can use to change the world.

BIBLIOGRAPHY

Adams, R. (2022). Guidance on political impartiality in English classrooms 'confusing' say teachers' unions. *The Guardian*, 17 February. Available at: www.theguardian.com/education/2022/feb/17/guidance-on-political-impartiality-in-english-classrooms-confusing-say-teachers-unions (Accessed 5 May 2022).

Adesioye, L. (2008). Is race a factor in sports success. *The Guardian*, 25 August. Available at: www.theguardian.com/commentisfree/2008/aug/25/race.olympics2008 (Accessed 12 December 2020).

Adichie, C.N. (2009). *The Danger of a Single Story*. TED Talk. Available at: www.youtube.com/watch?v=D9Ihs241zeg

Agarwal, P. (2020). *Sway: Unravelling Unconscious Bias*. London: Bloomsbury Sigma.

Ajayi, L. (2018). *Get Comfortable with Being Uncomfortable*. TED Talk. Available at: www.youtube.com/watch?v=QijH4UAqGD8

Alibhai, Z. (2022). Equalities minister says British Empire achieved 'good things' throughout rule. *The Independent*, 21 March. Available at: www.independent.co.uk/news/uk/politics/kemi-badenoch-british-empire-colonialism-b2040002.html

Andrews, K. (2022). *The New Age of Empire: How Racism and Colonialism Still Rule the World*. London: Penguin Books.

Anscombe, B., Kim, P., Verma, S. and Tanguturi, K (2021). How to spot Orientalism. *ArcGIS StoryMaps*. Available at: https://storymaps.arcgis.com/stories/7e57aa26b664437db8753e916ef7c39c

App, U. (2006). *Schopenhauer's Initial Encounter with Indian Thought*. Available at: https://download.uni-mainz.de/fb05-philosophie-schopenhauer/files/2020/01/2006_App_Initial%20Encounter.pdf (Accessed 26 April 2024).

Arthur, M. (2012). *Forgotten Voices of The Great War*. London: Random House.

Asare, J.G. (n.d.). Why the 'I don't see color' mantra is hurting your diversity and inclusion efforts. *Forbes*. Available at: www.forbes.com/sites/janicegassam/2019/02/15/why-the-i-dont-see-color-mantra-is-hurting-diversity-and-inclusion-efforts/?sh=51f891d02c8d (Accessed 12 April 2024).

Ashbee, R. (2021). *Curriculum: Theory, Culture and the Subject Specialisms*. Abingdon: Routledge.

Atkinson, H., Bardgett, S., Budd, A., Finn, M., Kissane, C., Qureshi, S., Saha, J., Siblon, J. and Sivasundaram, S. (2018). *Race, Ethnicity & Equality in UK History: A Report and Resource for Change*. [online] Royal Historical Society. Available at: https://blog.royalhistsoc.org/rhs-race-ethnicity/rhs-ree-publications/.

Bagalini, A. (2020). Colourism: How skin-tone bias affects racial equality at work. *World Economic Forum*. Available at: www.weforum.org/agenda/2020/08/racial-equality-skin-tone-bias-colourism/

Baglieri, S. and Lalvani, P. (2020). *Undoing Ableism: Teaching about Disability in K-12 Classrooms*. New York: Routledge.

Baker, M. (2012). Modernity/coloniality and Eurocentric education: Towards a post-occidental self-understanding of the present. *Policy Futures in Education*, 10(1): 4–22. https://doi.org/10.2304/pfie.2012.10.1.4

Baker, P. (2023). *Outrageous! The Story of Section 28 and Britain's Battle for LGBT Education*. London: Reaktion Books.

Bamberg, M. and Andrews, M. (2004). *Considering Counter Narratives: Narrating, Resisting, Making Sense*. Amsterdam: John Benjamins Publishing Company.

Barnes, C. (1992). *Disabling Imagery and the Media: An Exploration of the Principles for Media Representations of Disabled People the First in a Series of Reports*. The British Council of Organisations of Disabled People/Ryburn Publishing. Available at: https://disability-studies.leeds.ac.uk/wp-content/uploads/sites/40/library/Barnes-disabling-imagery.pdf

Batty, D. and Parveen, N. (2021). UK schools record more than 60,000 racist incidents in five years. *The Guardian*, 28 March. Available at: www.theguardian.com/education/2021/mar/28/uk-schools-record-more-than-60000-racist-incidents-five-years

Begum, S., Wylie, M., Anwari, H. and Hood, S. (2024). *Visualise: Race and Inclusion in Secondary School Art Education*. Runnymede Trust/Freelands Foundation. Available at: www.runnymedetrust.org/publications/visualise-race-and-inclusion-in-secondary-school-art-education (Accessed 8 April 2024).

Bhambra, G.K., Gebrial, D. and Nisancioglu, K. (2018). *Decolonising the University*. London: Pluto Press.

Bishop, R. (1990). Mirrors, windows and sliding glass doors. *Perspectives: Choosing and Using Books for the Classroom*, 6(3): ix–xi.

Bourdillon, H. and Bartley, P. (1988). Controversial Women. *Teaching History*, 52, 10–14.

Brandman, M. (2021). We'wha. *National Women's History Museum*. Available at: www.womenshistory.org/education-resources/biographies/wewha

Brandwatch (2019). The scale of transphobia online. Available at: www.brandwatch.com/reports/transphobia/

Brontë, C. (1847). *Jane Eyre*. London: Benediction Classics.

Brown, M., McNamara, G., O'Brien, S., Skerritt, C., O'Hara, J., Faddar, J., Cinqir, S., Vanhoof, J., Figueiredo, M. and Kurum, G. (2019). Parent and student voice in evaluation and planning in schools. *Improving Schools*, 23(1): 85–102. https://doi.org/10.1177/1365480219895167

Burgis, T. (2016). *The Looting Machine: Warlords, Oligarchs, Corporations, Smugglers, and the Theft of Africa's Wealth*. New York, NY: PublicAffairs.

Busby, E. (2018). White pupils at Bath school 'tied up and whipped black student for mock slave auction'. *The Independent*, 14 March. Available at: www.independent.co.uk/news/education/education-news/mock-slave-auction-black-student-white-pupils-bath-school-whipped-tied-up-a8255206.html

Camus, R (2015). *Le grand remplacement*. Plieux: Renaud Camus, Dl.

Carlsson Rex, H. and Trohanis, Z. (2012). *Making Women's Voices Count: Integrating Gender Issues in Disaster Risk Management: Overview and Resources for Guidance Notes (English)*. East Asia and the Pacific Region Sustainable Development Guidance Note

No. 0. Gender and Disaster Risk Management. Washington, DC: World Bank Group. Available at: http://documents.worldbank.org/curated/en/723731468234284901/ Making-womens-voices-count-integrating-gender-issues-in-disaster-risk-management-overview-and-resources-for-guidance-notes

Carter, R. (2019). Young people in the time of Covid-19: A fear and hope study of 18-24 year olds. Hope Charitable Trust. Available at: https://hopenothate.org.uk/ wp-content/uploads/2020/08/youth-fear-and-hope-2020-07-v2final.pdf

CDP (Center for Disaster Philanthropy) (n.d.). Women and girls in disasters. Available at: https://disasterphilanthropy.org/resources/women-and-girls-in-disasters/

Coe, R., Aloisi, C., Higgins. S. et al. (2014). *What Makes Great Teaching? Review of the Underpinning Research*. London: Sutton Trust.

Conan Doyle, A. (2009). *The Complete Sherlock Holmes*. Harmondsworth: Penguin.

Connell, R. (2007). *Southern Theory: The Global Dynamics of Knowledge in Social Science*. Cambridge: Polity.

Counsell, C. (2018a). Senior Curriculum Leadership 1: The indirect manifestation of knowledge: (A) curriculum as narrative. *The Dignity of the Thing*. Available at: https:// thedignityofthethingblog.wordpress.com/2018/04/07/senior-curriculum-leadership-1-the-indirect-manifestation-of-knowledge-a-curriculum-as-narrative/

Counsell, C. (2018b). Taking curriculum seriously. *Impact*, 4(September).

Craik, M.D. (1875). *The Little Lame Prince*. London: Ludgate Hill.

Crenshaw, K. (2020). Mapping the margins: Intersectionality, identity politics, and violence against women of color. In *On Intersectionality: Essential Writings*. New York: New Press.

Damus, O. (2021). Towards an epistemological alliance for the decolonization of knowledge of the global South and the global North. *UNESCO's Futures of Education Ideas LAB*. Available at: https://en.unesco.org/futuresofeducation/ideas-lab/damus-epistemological-alliance-decolonization-knowledge-global-South-global-North.

Dasgupta, N. (2011). Ingroup experts and peers as social vaccines who inoculate the self-concept: The stereotype inoculation model. *Psychological Inquiry*, 22(4): 231–46. https://doi.org/10.1080/1047840X.2011.607313

De Sousa Santos, B. (2014). *Epistemologies of the South: Justice against Epistemicide*. Abingdon and New York: Routledge.

Dhaliwal, V. (2023). The queer story of South Asia. *Brown History*. Available at: https:// brownhistory.substack.com/p/the-queer-story-of-south-asia (Accessed 12 April 2024).

Dowden, O. (2022). *Standing up for our values*. Available at: www.conservatives.com/ news/2022/standing-up-for-our-values (Accessed 15 April 2022).

Eberhardt, J.L. (2020). *Biased: Uncovering the Hidden Prejudice that Shapes What We See, Think, and Do*. London: Penguin Books.

educationhub.blog.gov.uk (2021). Black History Month: How Black history is taught in our schools. *The Education Hub*. Available at: https://educationhub.blog.gov. uk/2021/10/08/black-history-month-how-black-history-is-taught-in-our-schools/

education.nationalgeographic.org (n.d.). Exploring multiple perspectives. Available at: https://education.nationalgeographic.org/resource/exploring-multiple-perspectives/ (Accessed 28 March 2024).

EEF (Education Endowment Foundation) (n.d.). Implementation. Available at: https:// educationendowmentfoundation.org.uk/support-for-schools/implementation

Entine, J. (2001). *Taboo: Why Black Athletes Dominate Sports and Why We're Afraid to Talk About It*. New York: PublicAffairs.

explore-education-statistics.service.gov.uk (n.d.). Children looked after in England including adoptions. *Reporting year* 2021. Available at: https://explore-education-statistics.service.gov.uk/find-statistics/children-looked-after-in-england-including-adoptions#releaseHeadlines-tables

Faloyin, D. (2022). *Africa is Not a Country: Notes on a Bright Continent*. New York: W.W. Norton & Co.

Fanon, F. (1961). *The Wretched of the Earth*. Cape Town: Kwela Books.

Finney, N., Nazroo, J., Bécares, L., Kapadia, D. and Shlomo, N. (eds) (2023). *Racism and Ethnic Inequality in a Time of Crisis*. Bristol: Policy Press.

Ford, A. (2022). Why is 'powerful knowledge' failing to forge a path to the future of history education? *History Education Research Journal*, 19(1). https://doi.org/10.14324/herj.19.1.03

Ford, A. and Nigh, R. (2016). *The Maya Forest Garden*. Abingdon: Routledge.

Freire, P. (1970). *Pedagogy of the Oppressed*. New York: Bloomsbury Academic.

Gender Equality Toolbox (n.d.). Available at: www.gatesgenderequalitytoolbox.org/measuring-empowerment/agency/

Gilroy, P. (2002). *There Ain't No Black in the Union Jack: The Cultural Politics of Race and Nation*. London: Routledge.

Gopal, P. (2021). Why can't Britain handle the truth about Winston Churchill? *The Guardian*, 17 March. Available at: www.theguardian.com/commentisfree/2021/mar/17/why-cant-britain-handle-the-truth-about-winston-churchill

Gordon, R.A., Crosnoe, R. and Wang, X. (2013). Physical attractiveness and the accumulation of social and human capital in adolescence and young adulthood: Assets and distractions. *Monographs of the Society for Research in Child Development*, 78(6): 1–137.

Gove, M. (2009). *What is Education For?* Available at: www.thersa.org/globalassets/pdfs/blogs/gove-speech-to-rsa.pdf

Gove, M. (2013). The progressive betrayal. *Social Market Foundation*. Available at: www.smf.co.uk/michael-gove-speaks-at-the-smf/

Gregory, D. (2004). *The Colonial Present: Afghanistan, Palestine, Iraq*. Malden, MA: Blackwell.

Gresseth, G.K. (1975). The Gilgamesh epic and Homer. *The Classical Journal*, 70(4): 11–18.

Griffin, B.R. (2012). *Tales of Empire: Orientalism in Nineteenth-Century Children's Literature* Available at: https://digitalcommons.usf.edu/cgi/viewcontent.cgi?article=5253&context=etd

Hall, B.L. and Tandon, R. (2017). Decolonization of knowledge, epistemicide, participatory research and higher education. *Research for All*, 1(1): 6–19. doi:10.18546/RFA.01.1.02

Hammond, D. and Moyes, S. (2021). UK's 'wokest' headmaster ditches house names honouring national heroes after ex-pupil complains. *The Sun*. Available at: www.thesun.co.uk/news/14118543/woke-headmaster-ditches-national-heroes/ (Accessed 22 June 2022).

Harper, J.C. et al. (2022). An online survey of perimenopausal women to determine their attitudes and knowledge of the menopause. *Women's Health*, 18. doi:10.1177/17455057221106890

Hess, J. (2015). Decolonizing music education: Moving beyond tokenism. *International Journal of Music Education*, 33(3): 336–47. https://doi.org/10.1177/025576141 5581283

Hickel, J. (2018). *The Divide: A Brief Guide to Global Inequality and its Solutions*. London: Windmill Books.

Hicks, D. (2020). *Brutish Museums: The Benin Bronzes, Colonial Violence and Cultural Restitution*. London: Pluto Press.

Hill Collins, P. (2019). *Intersectionality as Critical Social Theory*. Durham, NC: Duke University Press.

Himmelstein, M.S., Young, D.M., Sanchez, D.T. and Jackson, J.S. (2014). Vigilance in the discrimination-stress model for Black Americans. *Psychology & Health*, 30(3): 253–67. https://doi.org/10.1080/08870446.2014.966104

Hirsch, A. (2018). *Brit(ish): On Race, Identity and Belonging*. London: Vintage.

Hirsch, E.D. (1989). *Cultural Literacy: What Every American Should Know*. Melbourne: Schwartz Pub.

Hogan, B. (2022). Why study dead white men? *Blog of the APA*. Available at: https://blog. apaonline.org/2022/05/09/why-study-dead-white-men/ (Accessed 12 April 2024).

Holmes, M.S. (2004). *Fictions of Affliction: Physical Disability in Victorian Culture*. Ann Harbor: University of Michigan Press.

Hooks, B. (1981). *Ain't I a Woman: Black Women and Feminism*. New York: Routledge, Cop.

houseofcommons.shorthandstories.com (n.d.). Teaching migration in the history curriculum. Available at: https://houseofcommons.shorthandstories.com/teaching-migration--in-the-history-curriculum/index.html (Accessed 12 April 2024).

Howard, K. and Hill, C. (2020). *Symbiosis: The Curriculum and the Classroom*. London: John Catt Educational.

Hübscher, A. (ed.) (1987). Letter to Johann Eduard Erdmann of 9 April, 1851; Arthur Schopenhauer: *Gesammelte Briefe*, Bonn: Bouvier, 1987: p. 261 (letter no. 251).

Hulan, H. (2017). Bury your gays: History, usage, and context. *McNair Scholars Journal*, 21(1): Article 6. Available at: https://scholarworks.gvsu.edu/mcnair/vol21/iss1/6

Institute of Race Relations (n.d.). Catching history on the wing. Available at: https://irr. org.uk/article/catching-history-on-the-wing/

Jennings, R. (2007). *A Lesbian History of Britain: Love and Sex Between Women Since 1500*. Oxford: Greenwood World Publishers.

Joseph, G.G. (1992). *The Crest of the Peacock*. London: Penguin Books.

Just Like Us (2021). Growing Up LGBT+: The impact of school, home and coronavirus on LGBT+ young people. Available at: https://www.justlikeus.org/wp-content/uploads/2021/11/Just-Like-Us-2021-report-Growing-Up-LGBT.pdf

Kahneman, D. and Tversky, A. (1979). Prospect theory: An analysis of decision under risk. *Econometrica*, 47(2): 263–91.

Kaufmann, M. (2018). *Black Tudors: The Untold Story*. London, England: Oneworld Publications.

Kara, B. (2020). *A Little Guide for Teachers: Diversity in Schools*. London: Corwin.

Kara, B. and Wilson, H. (2022). *Diverse Educators*. London: Legend Press.

Kendi, I.X. (2019). *How to be an Antiracist*. New York: One World.

Kenyon, J., Binder, J. and Baker-Beall, C. (2021). *Exploring the Role of the Internet in Radicalisation and Offending of Convicted Extremists*. Available at: https://assets.

publishing.service.gov.uk/government/uploads/system/uploads/attachment_data/
file/1017413/exploring-role-internet-radicalisation.pdf

Kerr, I.B. (2010). The myth of racial superiority in sports. *The Hilltop Review* 4(1).
Available at: https://scholarworks.wmich.edu/hilltopreview/vol4/iss1/4

Khalifa, M. (2016). How Disney projects orientalism through their movies. *Sail Magazine*.
Available at: https://sailemagazine.com/2016/11/how-disney-projects-orientalism-
through-their-movies/

Kimmerer, R.W. (2013). *Braiding Sweetgrass: Indigenous Wisdom, Scientific Knowledge and
the Teachings of Plants*. Minneapolis, MN: Milkweed Editions.

Kotter, J.P. (1996). *Leading Change*. Boston: Harvard Business School Press.

Krauss, J. (2018). Decolonising development – What, how, by whom and for whom?
Global Development Institute Blog. (Accessed 26 August 2021).

Ladau, E. (2021). *Demystifying Disability: What to know, what to say, and how to be an ally*.
California: Ten Speed Press, an imprint of Random House, a division of Penguin
Random House LLC.

LaFleur, G., Raskolnikov, M. and Kłosowska, A. (2021). *Trans Historical: Gender Plurality
Before the Modern*. Ithaca; London: Cornell University Press.

Lander, E. and Past, M. (2002). Eurocentrism, modern knowledges, and the 'natural'
order of global capital. *Nepantla: Views from South*, 3(2): 245–68. *Project MUSE* muse.
jhu.edu/article/23956

Le Bas, D. (2019). *The Stopping Places: A Journey Through Gypsy Britain*. London: Vintage.

Lee, C. (2023). *Pretended: Schools and Section 28: Historical, Cultural and Personal
Perspectives*. London: John Catt.

Local Government Act 1988 (c. 9). Section 28. Available at: www.legislation.gov.uk/
ukpga/1988/9/section/28/enacted (Accessed 4 December 2023).

Lorde, A. (1984). *Sister Outsider: Essays and Speeches*. S.L.: Penguin Books.

Luthra, P. (2022). 7 ways to practice active allyship. *Harvard Business Review*. Available at:
https://hbr.org/2022/11/7-ways-to-practice-active-allyship

MAI: Feminism & Visual Culture (2020). 'Where do you know from?': An exercise in
placing ourselves together in the classroom. Available at: https://maifeminism.com/
where-do-you-know-from-an-exercise-in-placing-ourselves-together-in-the-classroom/

Manley, N.W. (1973). Autobiography. *Jamaica Journal*, 7(1–2).

Marshall, T. (2016). *Prisoners of Geography: Ten Maps That Explain Everything About the
World*. New York, NY: Scribner.

Maylor, U., Read, B., Mendick, H., Ross, A. and Rollock, N. (n.d.). *The Early Stages of the
National Curriculum, Diversity and Citizenship in the Curriculum: Research Review*.
London: London Metropolitan University, The Institute for Policy Studies in
Education.

Medin, D., Lee, C.D. and Bang, M. (2014). Particular points of view. *Scientific American*,
311(4): 44–5. https://doi.org/10.1038/scientificamerican1014-44

Memmi, A. (2016). *The Colonizer and the Colonized*. London: Souvenir Press.

Mike (2023). Remembering the tuath. *Enough!* Available at: www.enough.scot/
remembering-the-tuath/ (Accessed 26 April 2024).

Milano, B. (2021). Racism, far before slavery. *Harvard Gazette*, 16 March. Available at:
https://news.harvard.edu/gazette/story/2021/03/cord-whitaker-discusses-black-
history-beyond-slavery/ (Accessed 28 March 2024).

Milem, J., Chang, M. and Lising, A. (2005). *Making Diversity Work on Campus: A Research-Based Perspective*. Available at: https://web.stanford.edu/group/siher/AntonioMilemChang_makingdiversitywork.pdf

Minkowski, W.L. (1992). Women healers of the middle ages: selected aspects of their history. *American Journal of Public Health*, 82(2), pp.288–295. doi:https://doi.org/10.2105/ajph.82.2.288.

Myatt, M. and Tomsett, J. (2021). *Huh: Curriculum Conversations between Subject and Senior Leaders*. London: John Catt.

Noble, S.U. (2018). *Algorithms of Oppression: How Search Engines Reinforce Racism*. New York: New York University Press.

Oakeshott, M. (1989). *Voice of Liberal Learning*. Indianapolis: Liberty Fund.

Office for National Statistics (2021). Religion, England and Wales. Available at: www.ons.gov.uk/peoplepopulationandcommunity/culturalidentity/religion/bulletins/religionenglandandwales/census2021

Office for National Statistics (ONS) (2023). Disability, England and Wales: Census 2021. Available at: https://www.ons.gov.uk/peoplepopulationandcommunity/healthandsocialcare/healthandwellbeing/bulletins/disabilityenglandandwales/census2021

Ofsted (2023). Education inspection framework. Available at: www.gov.uk/government/publications/education-inspection-framework/education-inspection-framework-for-september-2023

Ofsted (2024). Telling the story: The English education subject report. Available at: www.gov.uk/government/publications/subject-report-series-english/telling-the-story-the-english-education-subject-report

Olneck, M. (2001). Re-naming, re-imagining America: multicultural curriculum as classification struggle. *Pedagogy, Culture and Society*, 9 (3): 333–354.

Olusoga, D. (2016). *Black and British: A Forgotten History*. London: Picador.

Otele, O. (2020). *African Europeans: An Untold History*. London: Hurst & Company.

Oxford Royale Academy (2020). 600 EPQ ideas – The ultimate list for an A*. Available at: www.oxford-royale.com/articles/epq-ideas/

Panayi, P. (2020). Immigration and the making of British food. *The Historian*, 8 July.

Patel, I.S. (2021). *We're Here Because You Were There: Immigration and the End of Empire*. London: Verso.

Patnaik, U. and Patnaik, P. (2021). The drain of wealth. *Monthly Review*. Available at: https://monthlyreview.org/2021/02/01/the-drain-of-wealth/

Pearson (2020). *Diversity Inclusion in Schools*. Harlow: Pearson. Available at: www.pearson.com/content/dam/one-dot-com/one-dot-com/uk/documents/educator/schools/issues/inclusion/diversity-and-inclusion-in-schools-report.pdf

Piaget, J. (1976). Cognitive development in children: Piaget development and learning. *Journal of Research in Science Teaching*, 2: 176–86. https://doi.org/10.1002/tea.3660020306

Picq, M.L. and Tikuna, J. (2019). Indigenous sexualities: Resisting conquest and translation. *E-International Relations*. Available at: www.e-ir.info/2019/08/20/indigenous-sexualities-resisting-conquest-and-translation/

Pirchio, S., Passiatore, Y., Panno, A., Maricchiolo, F. and Carrus, G. (2018). A chip off the old block: Parents' subtle ethnic prejudice predicts children's implicit prejudice. *Frontiers in Psychology*, 9. doi:10.3389/fpsyg.2018.00110

Procter, A. (2019). *The Whole Picture: The Colonial Story of the Art in Our Museums and Why We Need To Talk About It*. London, UK: Cassell.

Promotion of National Unity and Reconciliation Act 34 of 1995, Available at: www. justice.gov.za/legislation/acts/1995-034.pdf (Accessed 24 April 2024).

Puttick, S. and Murrey, A. (2022). Parody tests for anti-racist and decolonial geography school teaching. *Decolonising Geography*. Available at: https://decolonisegeography. com/blog/2022/02/parody-tests-for-anti-racist-and-decolonial-geography-school-teaching/ (Accessed 10 April 2024).

Quayson, A. and Mukherjee, A. (2024). *Decolonizing the English Literary Curriculum*. Cambridge: Cambridge University Press.

Ramesh, R. (2007). India's secret history: 'A holocaust, one where millions disappeared...' *The Guardian*, 24 August. Available at: www.theguardian.com/ world/2007/aug/24/india.randeepramesh

Ramirez, J. (2022). *Femina: A New History of the Middle Ages Through the Women Written Out of It*. London: WH Allen.

Rauscher, L. and McClintock, J. (1997). Ableism curriculum design. In M. Adams, L.A. Bell and P. Griffen (eds), *Teaching for Diversity and Social Justice* (pp. 198–229). New York: Routledge.

Rhys, J. (1966). *Wide Sargasso Sea*. New York and London: W.W. Norton & Co.

Rutherford, A. (2020). *How to Argue With a Racist*. Experiment.

Said, E. (2004). *The Colonial Present: Afghanistan, Palestine and Iraq* . Philadelphia: Wiley-Blackwell.

Said, E.W. (1978). Introduction and Chapter 1 of *Orientalism*. Available at: https://sites. evergreen.edu/politicalshakespeares/wp-content/uploads/sites/33/2014/12/Said_full. pdf

Saini, A. (2018). *Inferior: How Science Got Women Wrong and the New Research that's Rewriting the Story*. Boston: Beacon Press.

Saini, A. (2019). *Superior: The Return of Race Science*. London: Fourth Estate Ltd.

Sanders, S. (2019). *From a Whisper to a Roar*. Available at: www.whisper2roar.org.uk/ wp-content/uploads/2020/02/Sue-Sanders.pdf (Accessed 12 April 2024).

Sanghera, S. (2021). *Empireland: How Imperialism has Shaped Modern Britain*. London: Viking.

Science and Technology Committee (n.d.). Diversity and inclusion in STEM. Available at: https://publications.parliament.uk/pa/cm5803/cmselect/cmsctech/95/report.html (Accessed 8 April 2024).

Shakespeare, T. (2018). *Disability: The Basics*. Abingdon: Routledge.

SikhNet (2009). Impact of WWI on Sikh soldiers based on their letters. Available at: www.sikhnet.com/news/impact-wwi-sikh-soldiers-based-their-letters

Singh, H. (2016). *The Rani of Jhansi: Gender, History, and Fable in India*. Delhi: Cambridge University Press.

Siollun, M. (2021). *What Britain Did to Nigeria: A Short History of Conquest and Rule*. London: Hurst & Co.

Sitholé, T., Crawley, H., Feyissa, D., Tapsoba, T.A., Meda, M.M., Sangli, G., Yeoh, S.G. and Phipps, A. (2022). The language of migration. *Zanj: The Journal of Critical Global South Studies*, 5(1/2): 14–26. https://doi.org/10.13169/ zanjglobsoutstud.5.1.0002

Sky News. (n.d.). Antisemitism 'rife' on social media platforms like Instagram and TikTok, research finds. Available at: https://news.sky.com/story/antisemitism-rife-on-social-media-platforms-like-instagram-and-tiktok-research-finds-12432690

Smithsonian (2019). Being antiracist. *National Museum of African American History and Culture.* Available at: https://nmaahc.si.edu/learn/talking-about-race/topics/being-antiracist

Spender, D. (1982). *Invisible Women.* London: Writers and Readers.

Stop Hate UK (2021). Transgender hate. Available at: www.stophateuk.org/about-hate-crime/transgender-hate/

Stryker, S. (2008). *Transgender History.* New York: Seal Press.

Tatum, B.D. (2017). *'Why Are All the Black Kids Sitting Together in the Cafeteria?' And Other Conversations about Race.* New York: Basic Books.

Tharoor, S. (2018). *Inglorious Empire: What the British did to India.* London: Penguin Books Ltd.

The Traveller Movement (2020). *Gypsy, Roma and Traveller Experiences in Secondary Education: Issues, Barriers and Recommendations.* Available at: https://wp-main.travellermovement.org.uk/wp-content/uploads/2021/09/GRT-in-Secondary-Education-2021.pdf

Thiong'o, N.W. (1986). *Decolonising the Mind: The Politics of Language in African Literature.* London: James Currey.

Thorndike, E.L. (1920). A constant error in psychological ratings. *Journal of Applied Psychology,* 4(1): 25–29. https://doi.org/10.1037/h0071663

Todd, J. (2019). Thinking beyond boundaries. *Teaching History,* 176 (Widening Vistas edn): 4–7.

Tomlinson-Gray, D. (2020). *Big Gay Adventures in Education.* Abingdon: Routledge.

Torres, E. (2020). What it means to center ourselves in conversation – and how to practice decentering instead. *The Good Trade.* Available at: www.thegoodtrade.com/features/decentering-yourself/

Travis, D.J. and Thorpe-Moscon, J. (2018). *Day-to-Day Experiences of Emotional Tax Among Women and Men of Color in the Workplace.* Catalyst.

Tuck, E. (2012). Decolonisation is not a metaphor. *Decolonization: Indigeneity, Education & Society,* 1(1): 1–40.

United Nations (1978). *Declaration on Race and Racial Prejudice.* Available at: www.un.org/en/genocideprevention/documents/atrocity-crimes/Doc.11_declaration%20on%20race%20and%20racial%20prejudice.pdf

Verso Books (2020). The souls of white folk: an essay by W.E.B. Du Bois on the imperial roots of American racism. Available at: https://www.versobooks.com/en-gb/blogs/news/4770-the-souls-of-white-folk

Visram, R. (2002). *Asians in Britain: 400 years of History.* London: Pluto Press.

Wansink, B., Akkerman, S., Zuiker, I. and Wubbels, T. (2018). Where does teaching multiperspectivity in history education begin and end? An analysis of the uses of temporality. *Theory & Research in Social Education,* 46(4): 495–527. https://doi.org/10.1080/00933104.2018.1480439

Weale, S., Bakare, L. and Mir, S. (2020). Calls grow for black history to be taught to all English school pupils. *The Guardian,* 8 June. Available at: www.theguardian.com/education/2020/jun/08/calls-mount-for-black-history-to-be-taught-to-all-uk-school-pupils

Weiss, A.I. (1991). Harold Bloom, The art of criticism No. 1. Available at: www.theparisreview.org/interviews/2225/the-art-of-criticism-no-1-harold-bloom

Wilkinson, M.L..N. (2013). Curriculum for cohesion: Bringing humanities to life Available at: https://eprints.soas.ac.uk/21011/1/CfC-Response-July-DfE-Draft-History-Curriculum-30.07.13.pdf

Wogg, M. (n.d.). *Romani Literature*. Roma and Travellers Team.

Wong, A. (2022). *Disability Visibility: First-person Stories From the Twenty-first Century*. New York: Vintage Books, a division of Penguin Random House LLC.

World Health Organization (2023). Traditional medicine has a long history of contributing to conventional medicine and continues to hold promise. Available at: www.who.int/news-room/feature-stories/detail/traditional-medicine-has-a-long-history-of-contributing-to-conventional-medicine-and-continues-to-hold-promise

www.education-uk.org (n.d.). Swann Report (1985). Available at: www.education-uk.org/documents/swann/swann1985.html

www.gov.wales (2024). *An anti-racist Wales*. Available at: www.gov.wales/anti-racist-wales (Accessed 12 April 2024).

www.imiscoe.org (n.d.). Taking decolonising seriously – the problem with migration studies. IMISCOE. Available at: www.imiscoe.org/news-and-blog/phd-blog/1121-taking-decolonising-seriously-the-problem-with-migration-studies#:~:text=In%20this%20short%20piece%2C%20taking (Accessed 12 April 2024).

www.science.org (n.d.). Migration, not conquest, drove Anglo-Saxon takeover of England. Available at: www.science.org/content/article/migration-not-conquest-drove-anglo-saxon-takeover-england

www.tes.com (n.d.). Michael Young: What we've got wrong about knowledge and curriculum. Available at: www.tes.com/magazine/teaching-learning/general/michael-young-powerful-knowledge-curriculum

Young, M. (2013). Overcoming the crisis in curriculum theory: a knowledge-based approach. *Journal of Curriculum Studies*, 45(2): 101–118. doi:https://doi.org/10.1080/00220272.2013.764505.

Young, M. and Muller, J. (2010). Three educational scenarios for the future: Lessons from the sociology of knowledge. *European Journal of Education*, 45(1): 11–27.

Young, M., Lambert, D., Roberts, C., et al. (2014) *Knowledge and the Future School: Curriculum and Social Justice*. London: Bloomsbury.

INDEX

Page numbers in *italics* relate to Figures and Tables.

ableism, 50–51, 84
Adams, R., 9
Adesioye, L., 113
Adichie, Chimamanda Ngozi, 77–78, 129
adoption and fostering, 36–37
Agarwal, P., 4
age and ageing, 34
agency, 52, 80, 82–83, *83*, 105–106, 117
Ajayi, L., 56
Alibhai, Z., 112
allyship, 12
Anscombe, B., 114–115
anti-racism, 12, 13–14
anti-Semitism, 7
  see also Holocaust
Apartheid, 97–98
App, U., 70
Arnold, Matthew, 24
Art teaching, 24–25, 50, 65, 72–73, 94
Arthur, M., 80
Asare, J.G., 14
attractiveness, 6
Aung Sang Suu Kyi, 104

Badenoch, Kemi, 112
Baglieri, S., 50
Baker, M., 68
Baker, P., 46
'balance sheet' approach, 111–112
Baldwin, James, 100–101
Bamberg, M., 50
Barnes, C., 109–110
Bartley, P., 44
Batty, D., 1
Bhambra, G.K., 22–23, 92
bias, assumptions and beliefs, 4–6
  see also prejudices
Bishop, R., 3
Black history, 2, 52, 105–106, 136
Bloom, H., 103
Bourdillon, H., 44
Brandman, M., 69
'Britishness,' 67, 89, 96, 139–140
Brontë, Charlotte, 84

Brown, M., 63
Burgis, T., 131

Çaglar, A., 92
Camus, R., 90
Carlsson Rex, H., 80–81
Carter, R., 6–7
case studies
  Geography, 129–131, *131*
  History, 119–122
  Languages, 132–134
  Mathematics, 126–128
  Music, 134–136
  Science, 122–126
Catalyst (organisation), 19
Center for Disaster
    Philanthropy (CDP), 80–81
change
  EEF implementation plan, 57–59, *58*
  Kotter's change model, 56–57, *57*
Churchill, Winston, 103
class, exploration using paired texts, *84*
Classics teaching, 82
classroom displays, 100
Coe, R., 63
Collins, P.H., 17
colonialism
  countering dominant narratives, 111–112
  and Orientalism, 114
  and parallel stories, 78, *83*
  and refugees, 97
  and role models, 101–102, 103
  see also decolonised curriculum;
      enslavement; Eurocentrism
colour blindness, 14
Colston, Edward, 103
Connell, R., 47–48
conspiracy theories, 6–7
Counsell, C., 28–29
Crenshaw, K., 17
cultural capital, 27–28
curriculum diversification
  commitments required, 141–142
  decolonisation, 2, 16, 17, 126, 128, 134

evaluation, 33–41, *33*, 59–60, *59*,
  119–120, 123
and knowledge schemas, 21–22
levels of diverse content in, 31, *32*, 139
levels of influence over, 22–26, *23*
monitoring and accountability, 60–63
in monocultural schools, 137–138
planning sequences, 31
and power, 26–29, *29*
purpose of (in general), 1–2
as window into worlds, 3
see also diversity, equality and inclusion
  (DEI)
Curriculum for Cohesion, 121

Damus, O., 47
Dance teaching, 93–94
Dasgupta, N., 99–100
De Sousa Santos, B., 28, 68
'dead lesbian syndrome,' 105
'dead white men' over-representation,
  102–103
decolonised curriculum, 2, 16, 17, 126,
  128, 134
DEI *see* diversity, equality and inclusion
  (DEI)
Dhaliwal, V., 69–70
disability
  ableism, 50–51, 84
  countering dominant narratives, 109–110
  curriculum audit, 34–35
  intersectionalities, 86, 101
  in literature, 50, *84*, 110, 138
  paired texts, *84*
  and role models, 101, 110
disasters (natural), and multiperspectivity,
  80–81
Diverse Educators community, 56
diversity, equality and inclusion (DEI)
  and critical thinking, 5
  diversity vs decolonisation, 16–17
  equality vs equity, 14–16, *15*
  key concepts and texts, 11–20, 64–65
  'literacy' in for teachers, 55–56
  and political impartiality, 8–9
  role of schools in (overview), 7–8, *8*
  web resources, 64
  see also curriculum diversification
Dowden, Oliver, 8–9
Drama teaching, 82
DT (Design and Technology) teaching, 74, 94
Du Bois, W.E.B., 122

East, 'othering,' 113–116
EEF (Education Endowment Foundation)
  implementation plan, 57–59, *58*

emotional tax, 19–20
encounter hierarchy, 44–45, 124
English teaching
  disabilities narratives, 50–51
  expanding the knowledge boundaries,
    70–71
  National Curriculum, 24
  paired texts, 84–86, *84*
  planning sequences, 31, 45
  subject support/resources, 64–65
  teacher subject knowledge development,
    63–64
  Western canonical lens, 103
  see also literature
enslavement, 1, 2, 68, *83*, 96, 105, 113,
  120, 136
Entine, J., 113
epistemologies, 28, 47–48, 68
  see also knowledge
equality, vs equity, 14–16, *15*
Equality Act 2010
  and curriculum evaluation, 33–34, 60, 123
  Protected Characteristics in, 33
equity, vs equality, 14–16, *15*
etymology, and migration, 93–95, 96
Eurocentrism, 21–22, *23*, 28–29, 47–48, 68,
  71, 72–74, 92
evaluation of the curriculum, 33–41, *33*,
  59–60, *59*
  case studies, 119–120, 123
  see also monitoring the curriculum and
    accountability
examinations, 25
Extended Project Qualification (EPQ), 86–87

Faloyin, D., 130
feudalism, across the globe, 71–72
Feyissa, Dereje, 92
Finney, N., 49
First World War, and multiperspectivity,
  78–80, 122
Food Technology teaching, 82, 94, 96
Ford, A., 27, 48
Freire, P., 52

gender discrimination and inequalities
  (societal), 15, 34, 43, 68, 69, 83, 101
Gender Equality Toolbox, 52
gender fluidity, 69–70, *84*
gender reassignment, 35–36
gender stereotyping, 125
Geography teaching
  case study, 129–131, *131*
  disciplinary questions, *30*
  expanding the knowledge boundaries,
    69, 72

and indigenous knowledge, 48
migration/movement, 91, *91*
multiperspectivity, 80–81, *81*
National Curriculum, 130
subject support/resources, 65, 130
Gibb, Nick, 89
Global South, under-representation, 47–48
see also Eurocentrism
'Goblin Market' (Christina Rosetti), 115
Gopal, P., 103
Gove, Michael, 3, 24, 25, 27
governors, 60
Gresseth, G.K., 71
Grey-Thompson, Dame Tanni, 101
Griffin, B.R., 115
group identity, 19
Gypsy communities, inclusion and
    representation, 49–50

Hall, B.L., 68
Halo Effect, 5–6
Harper, J.C., 34
Hayes, Helen, 89
HealthTalk website, 86
Hegel, G.W.F., 102
Heilman, Rosa, 117
Hess, J., 73
heteronormativity, 45–47, 84
Hill, Lee, 101–102
Hinkley, Angel (case study), 126–128
Hirsch, E.D., 27, 72
History teaching
    Black history, 2, 52, 105–106, 136
    case study, 119–122
    countering dominant narrative of
        colonialism, 111–112
    expanding the knowledge boundaries,
        71–72, 74
    Holocaust, 46, 49
    migration, 89, 91, 92, 96–97, 120
    multiperspectivity, 78–80, 122
    National Curriculum, 24, 89
    subject support/resources, 64–65, 79, 112
Hogan, B., 102
Holder, Nate, 136
Holmes, M.S., 50
Holocaust
    countering dominant narrative, 117
    in curriculum, 46, 49
    misinformation, 7
Hooks, B., 17–18
Hope Not Hate (charity), 6–7
Hulan, H., 105

immigration and immigrants *see* migration
impartiality, political, 8–9

indigenous people
    art, 73
    knowledge, 48–49, 68
    and multiperspectivity, 78, *81*
inequalities
    gender, 15, 34, 43, 68, 69, 83, 101
    race *see* racism
Institute of Physics, 125
intersectionality, 17–18, 86, 100–101
intertextuality, 70–71
Islamophobia, 18, 132
IT teaching, 82

Jane Eyre and *Wild Sargasso Sea*
    (paired texts), 84–85
Johnston, Natalie, 44, 51
    case study, 122–126
Judaism, countering dominant
    narrative, 117

Kahneman, D., 4
Kara, B., 80, 95
Kaufmann, M., 93
Kendi, I.X., 12, 13
Kerr, I.B., 113
Khalifa, M., 114
knowledge
    core and hinterland knowledge, 28–29, *29*
    expanding the boundaries of, 67–75
    indigenous knowledge, 48–49, 68
    and power, 26–29, *29*
    schemas, 21–22
    sequencing (encounter hierarchy), 44–45
    see also epistemologies
Kotter, J., 56–57, *57*
Krauss, J., 16

Lalvani, P., 50
language, offensive, 138
Language teaching *see* Modern Foreign
    Language teaching
leadership team, 60–61, 133, 138
Lee, C., 46
Leonardo Da Vinci, 106
LGBTQ+ people *see* sexuality
Linnaeus, Carl, 103–104, *104*, 125
literature
    expanding the knowledge boundaries, 70–71
    LGBTQ+ representation in, 133, 134
    paired texts, 84–86, *84*
    racism in, 84–85, *84*, 115–116, 117, 138
    representations of disability in, 50, *84*,
        110, 138
    see also English teaching
The Little Lame Prince and His Travelling Cloak
    (Diana Mulock Craik), 110

Lorde, A., 17
Luthra, P., 12
Lyfta (resource), 85–86

macro-level influences over curriculum,
    22–23, *23*
Mandela, Nelson, 97, 144
Manley, Norman, 79
marriage and civil partnership, curriculum
    audit, 37–38
Marshall, T., 130
maternity and pregnancy, 36–37, 86
Mathematics teaching
    case study, 126–128
    expanding the knowledge boundaries,
        73–74, 127–128
    language and etymology, 94–95
    storytelling in, 128
matriarchal societies, 68–69
McClintock, J., 50
Medin, D., 81–82
menopause, 34
meso-level influences over curriculum,
    23–25, *23*
micro-level influences over curriculum,
    23, 25–26
migration
    long history of, 90–91, 92–93
    and partition, 97–98
    and racism, 90, 92
    teaching about, 89–90, *90*, 91–92, *91*,
        93–98, 120
Milano, B., 52
Milem, J., 8
Mill, John Stuart, 3–4
Minkowski, W.L., 69
Misra, A., 111
Modern Foreign Language teaching
    case study, 132–134
    migration, 95
    multiperspectivity, 82
    pronouns, 36
Moffat, Luke (case study), 132–134
monitoring the curriculum and
    accountability, 60–63
    see also evaluation of the curriculum
monocultural schools, 137–138
multiperspectivity, 78–82
    see also parallel stories
Murrey, A., 72
'Muscular Christianity,' 110
Music teaching
    ABRSM examinations, 25
    case study, 134–136
    expanding the knowledge boundaries, 73,
        135–136
    migration, 94

Romani music, 49–50
    'world music,' 73, 135
Myatt, M., 61, 132

narratives, dominant (and countering)
    on colonialism, 111–112
    on disability, 109–110
    on Judaism, 117
    on neurodiversity, 116
    on Orientalism, 113–116
    on race and sport, 113
    on racism, 113–116, 125–126
    on sexuality, 116
National Curriculum
    Art, 24–25
    Black history in, 2
    diversity in, 23–25, 67
    English, 24
    Geography, 130
    History, 24, 89
    Science, 25, 51
    sexuality in, 46
    women in, 43–44, *44*
National Geographic, *81*
natural disasters, and multiperspectivity,
    80–81
Neal, Syreeta, 136
neurodiversity, 35, 116
Noble, S.U., 101

Oakeshott, Michael, 3
Of Mice and Men (John Steinbeck),
    50, *84*, 138
Ofsted, 27
oppression and victim narratives, 51–52,
    59–60, 83, 104–106, 117, 124
    see also agency
Orientalism, 113–116
'othering,' 18–19, 50, 91, 113–116
Own Voices, 85–86

paired musical works, 135, 136
paired texts, 84–86, *84*
Panayi, P., 96
parallel stories, 77–87, *83*, 122, 124
parenting (in curriculum), 36–37
parents
    consulting, 63, 119, 121
    prejudices of, 6
parodies, as teaching aide, 72
Parveen, N., 1
Patel, S., 34
Patnaik, U., 111
patriarchy, 43–44, 83, *83*
    see also gender discrimination and
        inequalities (societal)
PE and Sports Science teaching

and ableism, 51
countering dominant narrative of racial
   determinism, 113
expanding the knowledge boundaries, 75
role models, 101, 107
Pearson, 142–143
Piaget, J., 22
Picq, M.L., 69
Pirchio, S, 6
planning sequences, 31
political impartiality, 8–9
Politics teaching, 82
Pope, Jessie, 79, 80
power, and knowledge, 26–29, *29*
Powers, Jodie (case study), 129–131
pregnancy, 36–37, 86
prejudices
   parental, 6
   and stereotypes, 5
   and 'us-vs-them' mentality, 18–19
   vigilance against (emotional tax), 19–20
   see also bias, assumptions and beliefs;
      racism
Price, Florence, 135–136
PRIDE in schools, 133, 134
Prince, Mary, 105–106
Promotion of National Unity and
   Reconciliation Act 34 (1995) (South
   Africa), 97–98
pronouns
   and gender stereotyping, 125
   in Modern Foreign Language teaching, 36
PSHE (personal, social, health, economic)
   teaching
   countering dominant narratives of
      sexuality and neurodiversity, 116
   and disabilities, 50
   and matriarchal societies, 68–69
   and migration/movement, 91, *91*
   and Own Voices, 85
   and sexuality, 40
Puttick, S., 72

race
   countering dominant narratives, 113, 125
   curriculum audit, 38
   Linnaeus's classification, 103–104, *104*
   paired texts, *84*
race-gender intersectionality, 17–18, 100
race-sexuality intersectionality, 1, 100–101
racism
   anti-racism, 12, 13–14
   Apartheid, 97–98
   and biases/assumptions, 6
   and colonialism, 111–112
   countering dominant narratives, 113–116,
      125–126

definition and levels of, 12–13, *13*
in literature, 84–85, *84*, 115–116, 117, 138
and migration/immigration, 90, 92
offensive language, 138
Orientalism, 113–116
problematic figures, 102, 103–104,
   104, 125
resources, 126
in schools, 1, 4
on screen, 114
and search engines, 101
and single story of Africa, 77–78
and social media, 7
stories of, 79
see also colour blindness
Ramesh, R., 111
Rani of Jhansi, 106
Rauscher, L., 50
religions and beliefs/non-beliefs
   curriculum representation, 39,
      121–122, 132
   paired texts, *84*
Religious Studies teaching, 39, 70, 82, 117, 132
representative heuristics, 4–5
Rhys, Jean, 85
Rich, A., 46
Richards, Samir (case study), 119–122
role models, 99–107, 117
Roma communities, inclusion and
   representation, 49–50
Royal Historical Society, 121, 122
Rubin, G., 46

Said, E., 18, 113
Sanders, S., 30
Sanghera, S., 122
schemas, 21–22
school governors, 60
Schopenhauer, A., 70
Science teaching
   case study, 122–126
   contextualising white male-dominant
      narrative, 123–124
   disciplinary questions, *30*
   example selection, 124, 125
   expanding the knowledge boundaries, 69
   multiperspectivity, 81–82
   National Curriculum, 25, 51
   parallel stories, 124
   subject support/resources, 65, 125
   vacuum effect, 124–125
search engines, racialised and
   misogynistic, 101
The Secret Garden (Frances Hodgson
   Burnett), 110
Section 28, 46
senior leadership team, 60–61, 133, 138

sex and gender
  curriculum audit, 39–40
  language sensitivities, 126
  pronouns, 36, 125
  resources, 126
sexuality
  community attitudes towards teaching
    practices, 138–139
  countering dominant narratives, 116
  curriculum audit, 40–41
  and encounter hierarchy, 45
  expanding the knowledge boundaries, 69–70
  heteronormativity, 45–47, 84
  and intersectionality, 1, 17, 18, 101
  and marriage, 37–38
  paired texts, 84
  PRIDE in schools, 133, 134
  representation in Language learning,
    133–134
  and role models, 101, 104–105
  Section 28, 46
  'usualising,' 30, 31
Sheppard, Gemma (case study), 134–136
Shultz, Howard, 14
The Sign of Four (Arthur Conan Doyle), 115
Simmonds, Ellie, 101, 125
Singh, H., 106
Singh, Isher, 79
Siollun, M., 112
Sitholé, T., 92
slavery see enslavement
slogans, 14
Smithsonian, 13
social media, 6–7
Song Guan Yeoh, 92
Spender, D., 43
sports, racial stereotyping and counter-
  narratives, 113, 125
Sports Science teaching see PE and Sports
  Science teaching
Steele, C., 19
Stereotype Inoculation Model, 99–100
stereotype replication, in sports, 113
stereotype threat, 100
stereotyping, 5, 19, 125
  see also narratives, dominant
    (and countering); racism
stories
  in Mathematics teaching, 128
  parallel stories, 77–87, 83, 122, 124
students
  feedback on curriculum diversification,
    122, 134, 143
  role in curriculum diversification, 62–63, 142
subject knowledge development (teachers),
  63–64, 131, 136, 140
subject leaders, 61

Swann Report (1985), 67
Swift, Emma, 51
  case study, 122–126

Tandon, R., 68
Tatum, B.D., 19
teacher identity, and DEI work, 137
teacher training and development, 25–26,
  56, 63–65, 131, 136, 140
teachers, role in curriculum
  diversification, 61–62
teaching assistants, 62
TED Talks, 77–78, 129
Textiles teaching, 28, 29, 82
Thorndike, E.L., 5
Thorpe-Moscon, J., 19
Tikuna, J., 69
Todd, J., 120
tokenism, 8, 30–31, 126
Tomsett, J., 61
Torres, E., 56
transgender people, 35–36
transphobia, 35–36
Traveller communities, inclusion and
  representation, 49–50
Travis, D.J., 19
Trohanis, Z., 80–81
Tully, M., 92
Turing, Alan, 105
Tversky, A., 4

unconscious bias, 4
United Nations, Declaration on Race and
  Racial Prejudice, 12
'usualising' diversity, 30–31
'us-vs-them' mentality see 'othering'

vacuum effect, 124–125
victim narratives, 51–52, 59–60, 83,
  104–106, 117, 124
  see also agency

wall displays, 100
Warner, W., 46
water management systems (example), 72
Watson, James, 125
Weale, S., 2
weaving example (core vs hinterland
  knowledge), 28, 29
Welsh government, commitment to
  anti-racism, 13
Wild Sargasso Sea and Jane Eyre (paired texts),
  84–85
Windrush generation, 96–97
women
  and agency, 83
  and encounter hierarchy, 45, 124

expanding the knowledge boundaries,
68–69
First World War stories of, 79–80
gender discrimination and inequalities
(societal), 15, 34, 43, 68, 69, 83, 101
intersectionality, 17–18, 135–136
Jewish resistance workers, 117
maternity and pregnancy, 36–37, 86
matriarchal societies, 68–69
perspectives in science, 82

representation in curriculum, 18, 34,
40, 43–44, *44*, 68–69, 79–81, 124,
135–136
role models, 99, 101, 104, 105–106, 117
World Health Organization, 69

Yellow Face, 115
Young, M., 26–27

Zurosky, Eugenia, 16